THE
PASSION
TRANSLATION

12-LESSON STUDY GUIDE

THE BOOK OF
SONG OF
SONGS

Divine Romance

BroadStreet
P U B L I S H I N G

BroadStreet Publishing® Group, LLC
Savage, Minnesota, USA
BroadStreetPublishing.com

TPT: The Book of Song of Songs: 12-Lesson Bible Study Guide
Copyright © 2025 BroadStreet Publishing Group

9781424567669 (softcover)
9781424567676 (e-book)

Stock or custom editions of BroadStreet Publishing titles may be purchased in bulk for educational, business, ministry, fundraising, or sales promotional use. For information, please email info@broadstreetpublishing.com.

General editor: Brian Simmons
Managing editor: William D. Watkins
Writer: Christeena Kale

Design and typesetting | garborgdesign.com

Printed in the United States of America

25 26 27 28 29 5 4 3 2 1

Contents

From God's Heart to Yours

"God is love," says the apostle John, and "Everyone who loves is fathered by God and experiences an intimate knowledge of him" (1 John 4:7). The life of a Christ-follower is, at its core, a life of love—God's love of us, our love of him, and our love of others and ourselves because of God's love for us.

And this divine love is reliable, trustworthy, unconditional, other-centered, majestic, forgiving, redemptive, patient, kind, and more precious than anything else we can ever receive or give. It characterizes each person of the Trinity—Father, Son, and Holy Spirit—and so is as limitless as they are. They love one another with this eternal love, and they reach beyond themselves to us, created in their image with this love.

How do we know such incredible truths? Through the primary source of all else we know about the one God—his Word, the Bible. Of course, God reveals who he is through other sources as well, such as the natural world, miracles, our inner life, our relationships (especially with him), those who minister on his behalf, and those who proclaim him to us and others. But the fullest and most comprehensive revelation we have of God and from him is what he has given us in the thirty-nine books of the Hebrew Scriptures (the Old Testament) and the twenty-seven books of the Christian Scriptures (the New Testament). Together, these sixty-six books present a compelling and telling portrait of God and his dealings with us.

It is these Scriptures that *The Passionate Life Bible Study Series* is all about. Through these study guides, we—the editors and writers of this series—seek to provide you with a unique and welcoming opportunity to delve more deeply into God's precious Word, encountering there his loving heart for you and all the others he loves. God wants you to know him more deeply, to love him more devoutly, and to share his heart with others more frequently and freely. To accomplish this, we have based this study guide series on The Passion Translation of the Bible, which strives to "reintroduce the passion and fire of the Bible to the English reader. It doesn't merely convey the literal meaning of words. It expresses God's passion for people and his world by translating the original, life-changing message of God's Word for modern readers." It has been created to "kindle in you a burning desire to know the heart of God, while impacting the church for years to come."[1]

In each study guide, you will find an introduction to the Bible book it covers. There you will gain information about that Bible book's authorship, date of composition, first recipients, setting, purpose, central message, and key themes. Each lesson following the introduction will take a portion of that Bible book and walk you through it so you will learn its content better while experiencing and applying God's heart for your own life and encountering ways you can share his heart with others. Along the way, you will come across a number of features we have created that provide opportunities for more life application and growth in biblical understanding.

Experience God's Heart

This feature focuses questions on personal application. It will help you live out God's Word and to bring the Bible into your world in fresh, exciting, and relevant ways.

Share God's Heart

This feature will help you grow in your ability to share with other people what you learn and apply in a given lesson. It provides guidance on using the lesson to grow closer to others and to enrich your fellowship with others. It also points the way to enabling you to better listen to the stories of others so you can bridge the biblical story with their stories.

The Backstory

This feature provides ancient historical and cultural background that illuminates Bible passages and teachings. It deals with then-pertinent religious groups, communities, leaders, disputes, business trades, travel routes, customs, nations, political factions, ancient measurements and currency...in short, anything historical or cultural that will help you better understand what Scripture says and means.

 ## Word Wealth

This feature provides definitions for and other illuminating information about key terms, names, and concepts, and how different ancient languages have influenced the biblical text. It also provides insight into the different literary forms in the Bible, such as prophecy, poetry, narrative history, parables, and letters, and how knowing the form of a text can help you better interpret and apply it. Finally, this feature highlights the most significant passages in a Bible book. You may be encouraged to memorize these verses or keep them before you in some way so you can actively hide God's Word in your heart.

 ## Digging Deeper

This feature explains the theological significance of a text or the controversial issues that arise and mentions resources you can use to help you arrive at your own conclusions. Another way to dig deeper into the Word is by looking into the life of a biblical character or another person from church history, showing how that man or woman incarnated a biblical truth or passage. For instance, Jonathan Edwards was well known for his missions work among native American Indians and for his intellectual prowess in articulating the Christian faith, Florence Nightingale for the reforms she brought about in healthcare, Irenaeus for his fight against heresy, Billy Graham for his work in evangelism, Moses for the strength God gave him to lead the Hebrews and receive and communicate the law, and Deborah for her work as a judge in Israel. This feature introduces to you figures from the past who model what it looks like to experience God's heart and share his heart with others.

The Extra Mile

While The Passion Translation's notes are extensive, sometimes students of Scripture like to explore more on their own. In this feature, we provide you with opportunities to glean more information from a Bible dictionary, a Bible encyclopedia, a reliable Bible online tool, another ancient text, and the like. Here you will learn how you can go the extra mile on a Bible lesson. And not just in study either. Reflection, prayer, discussion, and applying a passage in new ways provide even more opportunities to go the extra mile. Here you will find questions to answer and applications to make that will require more time and energy from you—if and when you have them to give.

As you can see above, each of these features has a corresponding icon so you can quickly and easily identify them.

You will find other helps and guidance through the lessons of these study guides, including thoughtful questions, application suggestions, and spaces for you to record your own reflections, answers, and action steps. Of course, you can also write in your own journal, notebook, computer document, or other resource, but we have provided you with space for your convenience.

Also, each lesson will direct you toward the introductory material and numerous notes provided in The Passion Translation. There each Bible book contains a number of aids supplied to help you better grasp God's words and his incredible love, power, knowledge, plans, and so much more. We want you to get the most out of your Bible study, especially using it to draw you closer to the One who loves you most.

Finally, at the end of each lesson you'll find a section called "Talking It Out." This contains questions and exercises for application that you can share, answer, and apply with your spouse, a friend, a coworker, a Bible study group, or any other individuals or groups who would like to walk with you through this material. As Christians, we gather together to serve, study, worship, sing, evangelize, and a host of other activities. We grow together, not just on our own. This section will give you ample opportunities to engage others with some of the content of each lesson so you can work it out in community.

We offer all of this to support you in becoming an even more faithful and loving disciple of Jesus Christ. A disciple in the ancient world was a student of her teacher, a follower of his master. Students study, and followers follow. Jesus' disciples are to sit at his feet and listen and learn and then do what he tells them and shows them to do. We have created *The Passionate Life Bible Study Series* to help you do what a disciple of Jesus is called to do.

So go.

Read God's words.

Hear what he has to say in them and through them.

Meditate on them.

Hide them in your heart.

Display their truths in your life.

Share their truths with others.

Let them ignite Jesus' passion and light in all you say and do.

Use them to help you fulfill what Jesus called his disciples to do: "Now wherever you go, make disciples of all nations, baptizing them in the name of the Father, the Son, and the Holy Spirit. And teach them to faithfully follow all that I have commanded you. And never forget that I am with you every day, even to the completion of this age" (Matthew 28:19–20).

And through all of this, let Jesus' love nourish your heart and allow that love to overflow into your relationships with others (John 15:9–13). For it was for love that Jesus came, served, died, rose from the dead, and ascended into heaven. This love he gives us. And this love he wants us to pass along to others.

Why I Love the Book of Song of Songs

Among the vast tapestry of literature, few works can match the ethereal beauty, profound depth, and timeless relevance of the Song of Songs. As a reader who has immersed himself in its verses time and again, I am spellbound by its unique allure. This divine allegory, penned by Solomon, is the sweetest song of the ages, and it has captured my heart.

The Song of Songs unravels the breathtaking journey of the Shulamite, an allegorical figure whose tale transcends mere mortal romance. This narrative speaks to the core of human longing, desire, and ultimate fulfillment. Through the song's verses, we witness the tender wooing, the passionate pursuit, and the consummation of love—a journey that resonates deeply with every follower of Jesus.

Yet, beyond its surface narrative, the Song of Songs unveils a deeper truth, one that transcends the realms of earthly love. It is a divine parable that mirrors the journey of every yearning follower of Jesus—a path of surrender, intimacy, and transformation. In its verses, we see the echoes of Christ's relentless pursuit of his beloved, drawing her closer to himself with each tender whisper.

What sets the Song of Songs apart is its unparalleled depiction of love—both human and divine. It is a symphony of passion, desire, and devotion woven into the very fabric of its eight chapters. As the Shulamite declares her love for her beloved, affirmation and encouragement echo through the ages, resonating with the bride of Christ in every generation.

The Song of Songs is not just a literary masterpiece but a divine invitation—a call to the depths of the heart, where Christ yearns to reside. It is a sacred text that doesn't just touch the soul but also stirs the embers of love and devotion within us. In its verses, we hear the gentle whispers of the Divine Lover, beckoning us to a deeper intimacy and union with himself.

When I contemplate the Song of Songs, I am struck by its universal relevance and profound influence. It is a beacon of hope in a world marred by brokenness and despair—a testament to the power of true love, both earthly and heavenly, to redeem, restore, and renew. In its pages, I find comfort, inspiration, and a glimpse of the divine romance that awaits us all.

I love the Song of Songs because it reveals the boundless love of our Savior—a love that pursues us relentlessly, drawing us ever closer to himself. It is a divine allegory nestled in the heart of our Bible, inviting us to embark on a journey of love and intimacy that transcends time and space. May we heed its call, allowing it to penetrate the depths of our being and transform us into the radiant bride of Christ.

So if you're seeking a love story like no other, look no further than the Song of Songs. It is a masterpiece of divine romance, waiting to unfold its mysteries and captivate your heart. This beautiful study guide will be a light shining on the pages of the Song of Songs. I know you're going to love it!

Brian Simmons

LESSON 1

The Heart of the King for His Bride

(1:1)

Most believers have a deep longing to understand the heart of their Savior Jesus. We pour over the Gospels, studying every word carefully to glean a more fully developed picture of the one who gave his life for ours, the one who promises an eternity of abiding together in perfect unity. However, sometimes in our Christian walk, this God-man who is our heavenly Bridegroom can seem distant from our present reality.

If you have ever longed to read the thoughts and feelings of Jesus for his church, for his bride, and for yourself specifically, the Song of Songs will become a healing balm to your soul. It is filled with words of encouragement, words of adoration, and words of transformation coming directly from the heart of a King for his bride. We will see in our study how deeply this book has touched many believers throughout history. It has been termed the "Holy of Holies" of Scripture because reading it can bring you into the very presence of God. And in his glory, you can experience the fullness of his abiding love.

The book of Psalms is full of exhortations regarding the stead-fast love of God that will never fail us. The Song of Songs, on the other hand, is the written expression of his steadfast, abiding love for his beloved. In the song, we find a Bridegroom who never stops loving, encouraging, hoping, or believing in his beloved—independent of the season in which she finds herself. The Song of Songs describes every season that we will encounter as Christians and shows us the steadfast love of God pervading every storyline.

Through the ages, the Song of Songs has been subject to many interpretations, with some interpreters seeing it as Hebrew love poetry, others as wisdom literature, and still others as a how-to guide for romance and marriage. Despite the different approaches to this book, Hebrew rabbis and the early Christian church fathers defended the inclusion of this book in their respective canon of holy books because it represents the heart of God for his people.

A Christian today can receive the impartation of this love story of God for his beloved bride through the study of this book. Held within the mysteries of the Song of Songs is the transformation of the desert wilderness to the secret garden that will feed the nations. The story begins with a broken-hearted, sunburned shepherd girl and ends with a passionate, fiery, beloved wife who is taking new territory for their kingdom.

❤ EXPERIENCE GOD'S HEART

This study is an invitation to delve into the heart of the Bridegroom King, your Savior Jesus Christ, and allow his love to transform your life. We will experience moments in Scripture that will take our breath away as we consider God's profound love for his people. As we begin this journey, let's celebrate how God has already shown his heart of love toward us.

- *Was there a time in your life when you tangibly felt God's love? Describe what happened in you and through you.*

- *How did this experience change your understanding of God?*

- *How did this experience change your understanding of yourself?*

♥ SHARE GOD'S HEART

As we progress through the song, we will see that sharing what we experience and learn about the love of God is one of the simplest forms of sharing the good news of the gospel. While most of us might balk at preaching a gospel message in a public square, we do not find it difficult to share with a friend or family member a story about a loving God.

- *With whom do you share stories of God's steadfast love?*

- *Who in your life needs to experience unconditional love? How can you share a story of your experience of God's love so it may become healing for them?*

- *What activities in your natural weekly rhythms allow for conversations about God's goodness with your friends and family?*

Authorship

The writer of the Song of Songs introduces the book with this verse: "The most amazing song of all, by King Solomon." Because of this introduction, the Song of Songs is traditionally considered to have been authored by King Solomon sometime during the middle of the tenth century BC. However, some of the geographic references in the song could allow for a compilation of poetry over centuries.[2] For the purposes of this study, we will follow the traditional acceptance of King Solomon as the author.[3]

- *Read 1 Kings 3:5–12 and then answer the following questions:*

  What did God ask of Solomon?

  What was Solomon's reply?

  Did God give Solomon his request? If so, why?

- *Now read 1 Kings 4:29–32 and provide answers to the following questions:*

  What did these verses reveal to you about the wisdom of Solomon?

  How many proverbs did Solomon speak?

How many songs did he write?

Of all of Solomon's songs and proverbs, what we know as the Song of Songs is titled "The most amazing song of all." The Song of Songs was considered the most profound writing from the wisest man to walk the earth—until Jesus Christ, that is.

Interpretation Matters

Interpretation involves discovering the true intended meaning of a text, not simply what it says. For example, when Jesus said, "I am the Way, I am the Truth, and I am the Life" (John 14:6), what did he mean by "Way," by "Truth," and by "Life"? When we read these words, we tend to interpret them within our twenty-first-century culture and language. To understand what Jesus truly meant, we must look more closely at what those words meant in his context and language. Perhaps his message contained cultural inferences that those present would have understood and we might have missed. This is true for every Scripture passage and is especially important when studying the Song of Songs. We need to observe what the passage says and interpret what it means before we can begin to grasp how to apply it.

- *Why do you think that the interpretation phase of Bible study matters?*

- *Why is it not enough to simply notice what a passage says?*

- *Why is it important to also know what it means (its interpretation)?*

- *What other Scripture passages can you identify for which the cultural context impacts their meaning?*

Historical Interpretations

A tension has existed throughout the ages regarding how to interpret the Song of Songs. It is Hebrew love poetry that is filled with imagery describing the relationship between a king and his bride. Should we take this book literally? Or is it an allegory? Indeed, at various times in Hebraic and Christian history, some have argued for its removal from both the Christian and Hebrew holy books of Scripture. In each case, those prevailed who held the view that this book is an allegory that describes the love of God for his people, and thus the book has remained in the holy books.

As Father Juan G. Arintero (1860–1928) wrote in the introduction to his commentary on the Song of Songs, "The whole Judaic and Christian tradition is in perfect accord in recognizing the spiritual and mystical sense of this wonderful Song, always seeing in it the most eloquent testimony of the tender love and infinite bond linking God with His chosen people, and especially with those happy and privileged souls who receive the grace to respond to Him."[4]

The Natural Interpretation

Many modern commentators or Bible teachers will interpret the song from a more literal perspective, describing God's endorsement of human sexuality. When asked about their study of the Song of Songs, many will respond that their only exposure to it in church was at a marriage retreat.

Brian and Candice Simmons wrote in their commentary on the Song of Songs, "Although it is possible to glean some help through the metaphors and symbols of this interpretive model, it comes far short of reflecting the fullness of God's beauty within the Song of Songs. Keep in mind that Solomon had multiple wives and concubines, affairs with women who were not his wife. To make Solomon's greatest song simply one of his many polygamous affairs is not a perfect model in which to interpret the Song of Songs. Indeed, if that is the true way to view his book, making human sexuality the highest song, the greatest song ever composed by the wisest man on earth, we are left wanting more."[5]

- *What interpretive approach to the Song of Songs have you heard or been taught?*

- *What are some of the strengths and weaknesses of this approach?*

Jewish Historical Perspective

One of the earliest mentions of the Song of Songs occurs in the Babylonian Talmud in AD 137. A prominent Jewish rabbi named Akiva ben Joseph was arguing for the song to remain a part of holy Scripture. To answer the question of whether to remove the book from the canon, he wrote, "Heaven forbid! No Jew ever disputed the sanctity of the Song of Songs, [that he should say] it does not defile the hands; for all the ages are not equal to the day when the Song of Songs was given to Israel. For all the Writings are sacred, but the Song of Songs is the most sacred of all."[6]

The Song of Songs is an essential part of the Jewish tradition, revealing God's love for and devotion to the Jewish people. Even to this day, portions of the song are recited in preparation for the Sabbath each week. The Jews consider it one of the most sacred parts of Scripture and recite it during their observance of the Passover, the holiest time in the Hebrew calendar. During the commemoration of the Passover, Jews pray multiple times, "May He kiss me with His kisses" from the Song of Songs.[7]

- *Read through the short eight chapters of the Song of Songs, putting yourself in the sandals of an ancient Jewish Israelite, seeing the imagery as much as possible as a description of God's love for his chosen people.*

  What did you experience while reading the book that helps you appreciate why the Jewish people have held it with such reverence?

  What are your initial impressions of this book?

  Did any passages in particular catch your attention? Which ones?

Christian Historical Perspective

The early church fathers primarily offered an allegorical interpretation of the Song of Songs. The earliest writings on the subject date back as far as the church father Origen in the mid AD 200s. Origen brought forth the bridal paradigm of the "wedding" song. Pope Gregory the Great wrote his own commentary on the song sometime between 594 and 598. He followed the tradition of Origen, using an allegorical interpretation of the song. In his introduction, Pope Gregory was emphatic that the song was about union with God, not erotic human love. He also cross-referenced other Scripture passages to interpret the song.[8]

Other early church voices who wrote about the significance of the Song of Songs include Bede the Venerable (672–735), William of Saint Thierry (1075–1148), and Bernard of Clairvaux (1090–1153).[9]

With the Protestant Reformation came the Geneva Bible in 1560, translated by William Tyndale. His introduction of the Song of Songs clearly states the text represents the Bridegroom Jesus Christ and that within the text is the expression of his perfect love for the bride, his church. Tyndale wrote that Christ has sanctified and made his spouse holy, imparting to her "His pure bounty and grace without any of her deservings." The love of Christ for his church is not dependent upon her earning it or becoming worthy of it. He describes a bride who is found without "any spot or blemish" and who is "inflamed with love of Christ."[10]

Charles Spurgeon (1834–1892), a Reformed Baptist preacher from the Victorian era, gave fifty-two sermons on the Song of Songs. His collection of sermons is a treasure trove of revelation about the love of God for his bride. The following excerpt from a sermon he gave on January 23, 1859, at his Metropolitan Tabernacle in Newington, England, describes his thoughts on how important the Song of Songs is to any Christian believer who is willing to plunge its depths:

> When the Christian is nearest to heaven,
> this is the book he takes with him! There are
> times when he would even leave the Psalms
> behind, when standing on the borders of
> Canaan, when he is in the land of Beulah
> and he is just crossing the stream, and can
> almost see his Beloved through the rifts of
> the storm cloud—then it is he can begin to

sing Solomon's Song! This is about the only book he could sing in heaven, but for the most part, he could sing this through, still praising Him who is everlasting lover and friend.[11]

• *Reflect on your reading of the Song of Songs.*

Are you able to see Christ as the lover of his bride in the Song of Songs? If so, write down one or two things you noticed in the song that support your understanding.

Missional Perspective

The Song of Songs has an interesting history in the mission's community. The Shulamite journey in the song culminates with the bride taking the bridegroom to the henna fields, or the dark, wilderness areas. Studying the Song of Songs will give the missionary a biblical roadmap for reaching the lost.

A well-known and celebrated missionary to China, Hudson Taylor (1832–1905), released his personal commentary on the Song of Songs, entitled *Union and Communion*. In his commentary, he equated the reality of the song with abiding in Christ and experiencing all his fullness.[12]

Richard Wurmbrand (1909–2001), the founder of *Voice of the Martyrs*, also released his own commentary on the Song of Songs, called *The Sweetest Song*. In his commentary, he weaves the stories of those who gave all for the gospel through the verses of the song. He points to the practical uses and effectiveness of the song in the darkest of places. So many of the martyrs uttered, "I am my beloved's, and he is mine" at their last.[13]

- *Now reflect on how the Song of Songs could help a believer who, day after day, serves in the field of missions.*

  How could the study of the song help prepare them for the mission field?

  How could the song prepare them for hardship during their service? Might it inspire them to push through all the obstacles they encounter because of Christ's great love for them?

  How might the song impact their approach toward unbelievers? Would it help them see unbelievers as future brides-to-be, destined to be the beloved of Christ although they may not know him yet?

Perspectives of This Study

This study will follow the allegorical interpretation of the song rather than a literal or natural interpretation. We will follow the path of many great theologians who have gone before us to discover through this poetry the heart of God toward his people, the heart of the Bridegroom Jesus Christ for his bride.

We will also approach the song as one unified piece of poetry, one story, rather than as a collection of songs. This will allow us to see major and minor themes that weave throughout the book.

We will primarily use the cross-referencing approach for interpretation, allowing the Bible to interpret the Bible. The Song of Songs is filled with imagery from nature: dove's eyes, pomegranates, foxes, lilies, apple trees, and more. Many teachers of the song use attributes found in nature to explain the spiritual meaning of these passages. To understand the spiritual significance of "dove's eyes," for example, they will look to attributes of doves. Dove's eyes are fixed; they do not rotate. And doves mate for life. Teachers extrapolate spiritual meaning from these physical attributes.

This is a valid approach for interpreting the imagery in the song, but it can fall short compared to the meaning that we can find by instead looking at the same imagery in other Scripture verses. As much as possible, we will use the cross-referencing approach for interpretation. We will look for that same imagery in other verses of the Bible and consider what understanding that may add to the verse we are studying. For example, the dove symbolizes the Holy Spirit in Scripture. In this light, we can read John 1:32, where the Holy Spirit descended upon Jesus as a dove. We can then consider what this passage of Scripture teaches us about the Holy Spirit's work in us.

Finally, we will study the song for a personal application in our daily lives as Christians rather than a corporate interpretation for the body of Christ at large or God's people. While each of these applications is useful, for purposes of this study, we will focus on our personal relationship with Jesus in the context of spiritually abiding with him.

 THE EXTRA MILE

Brian and Candice Simmons wrote a commentary on the song entitled *The Sacred Journey*. This commentary is a wonderful companion for this Bible study. Consider getting their commentary and using it as a parallel resource throughout our journey through the Song of Songs.

Talking It Out

Since Christians grow in community, not just in solitude, every "Talking It Out" section contains questions you may want to discuss with another person or in a group. Here are the exercises for this lesson.

1. Prior to beginning this study, what was your experience with the Song of Songs? Have you studied it in a church or small group setting? Or on a personal level? And what form of interpretation was used?

2. What was surprising or interesting to you in the overview of the song in the history of Hebrew and Christian interpretation?

3. Have you ever considered Jesus as the Bridegroom? How would you like to grow in your relationship with God through this study?

4. Has your impression of the Song of Songs changed after reading this lesson? If so, in what way?

5. What are you most looking forward to in this study? What are you hoping to experience in this process?

LESSON 2

Let Him

(1:2–5)

The opening act within the song, in many ways, sets the stage for the entire drama. In just a handful of verses, the prayers of the Shulamite initiate a response by the bridegroom, which plays out over the entire book. He guides her into the restored life that she seeks. By the end of the last chapter of the book, our Shulamite lives a new reality that reflects everything she longed for in this first chapter and far more than she imagined.

- *Before beginning the lesson, read Song of Songs 1:2–5 to understand the overall context. What verses or phrases stood out to you? Why?*

Key Themes

The overarching theme of the song is the transformational healing power of love. The story begins with a sunburned, weary shepherd girl who has lost her first love in the hard work of tending the flock. She is a common woman who has captured the heart of a king. The king continually expresses his love for her until her shame, fear, doubt, and self-loathing all disappear. They are replaced with joy, peace, acceptance, and courage. As she learns to live within the shade of his grace, she blossoms into the fullness of her identity and calling.

The song weaves many subtle threads throughout the story. A prominent one is the restoration of a garden that has been lost to disarray—a nod to the garden of Eden restored. Another is the bringing of light into the darkness by the bride as she arises into her destiny and fullness of identity—a foreshadowing of the church whose light cannot be hidden. And finally, an invitation to a hilltop where the greatest sacrifice of love is laid down—an invitation to meet the King of kings on Calvary and let our lives become a living sacrifice for his glory.

These themes are just a few that we find in the text. Many more are awaiting your discovery.

- *In your reading of the song, did any specific imagery feel significant to you? Which one? What do you believe it represents?*

Key Figures

The song has four key figures. As we make our way through the book, we will connect each of these figures to our personal journey with Jesus, our Bridegroom.

The Shulamite: The Shulamite is the shepherd girl who becomes a queen. In the broadest interpretation, the Shulamite represents God's people, or his church, the bride. For the purposes of this study, we will take a more personal approach. As you read through the text, put yourself in the voice of the Shulamite. Make the same requests of the Bridegroom-King that she makes and wait expectantly for his response in your life.

- *Read the first TPT footnote for Song of Songs 1:2 regarding the word "Shulamite."*

   Now explain the connection between the Shulamite's name and Solomon's.

   Do you see yourself as the true likeness of Jesus on the earth? If so, how? If not, what hinders this thought?

The King (Solomon): Solomon is the king in the song. For our study, he will represent Jesus Christ, our true King of kings. As you read the words of love and encouragement of the king for his beloved throughout the song, listen for the voice of Jesus whispering the same words over you.

- *What were your observations of the Bridegroom-King during your initial reading of the song?*

- *How would you describe your current relationship with the Bridegroom Jesus? Do you feel close to him? Or does he seem far off?*

- *How do you most closely connect with him? As a Savior? As a friend? As your life partner? Explain.*

- *What could an abiding relationship with Jesus in your daily life look like?*

Friends or Brides-to-be: The Shulamite is followed through the story by a group of close friends whom other translations often refer to as the "Daughters of Jerusalem" or the "Daughters of Zion." They were captivated by her love story and kept a close eye on her interactions with the king. They tended to enter the story when the Shulamite was fully overcome with love or searching for her beloved. These friends play a significant role. They help us understand that our experiences with the king don't affect us in isolation but also influence those who are close to us. Just like the Shulamite, you have friends who are following your spiritual journey as you grow closer to Jesus. At the end of the song, these brides-to-be begin their own Shulamite journey.

- *What are your observations of the friends or brides-to-be?*

Overseers: The overseers are the spiritual leaders in the life of the Shulamite (3:3; 5:7). Some translations refer to them as the "Watchmen." In the story, we will encounter two types of overseers. The first led the Shulamite back to her beloved when she lost sight of him. The second type made a difficult situation even worse by their thoughtless and harmful actions. Believers often experience a mix of both throughout their Christian walk. Whether intentionally or not, church leadership can hurt us. The Song of Songs offers some interesting insight into how to respond and heal from these experiences. It also offers a strategy for identifying healthy spiritual leaders versus unhealthy ones.

- *Reread 3:3 and 5:7 and some of the surrounding verses to gain the context. What are some of your observations of the overseers?*

The Setting

As we move through the story of our beloved Shulamite and her Shepherd-King, we will encounter many settings, almost like scenes in a play. The setting in which each interaction occurs is a significant part of the story. The song begins in a shepherd's field and quickly moves into the king's chambers. We will find our Shulamite under an apple tree, in a lily-filled valley, a wine cellar, the city streets, and green pastures. She will go to the henna fields and the orchards. We will see the transformation of her inner garden throughout the journey. She will experience mountains of separation and the ultimate destination—the "mountains of fragrant spice," where she will experience divine union with her Beloved (8:14). As each setting changes, we will consider the importance of the location to the specific interaction.

- *What places in your life do you feel especially close to God? Do you have a special spot that you return to frequently when you are longing for more of his presence? If so, where is it? What is it about that place that plays this special role in your life?*

• *Has God ever used the natural setting around you to reveal something about what he is like? Or about his steadfast love for you? If so, where was it, and what did he reveal to you?*

Let Him Kiss Me

The opening verses in the song set a foundation for the rest of the story. Even the first two words of the song, "Let him," can be considered one of the most critical lessons imparted by the Shulamite journey. Let's look closely at the first few verses.

• *Read Song of Songs 1:2, including the TPT footnotes for that passage.*

> *How would you compare the cry of your heart for more of God to that of the Shulamite in this verse? Are you desperate for more of God? Are you feeling distant from him? If so, why?*

> *How does this verse relate to 1 John 4:19?*

# EXPERIENCE GOD'S HEART

The TPT footnote 'c' for Song of Songs 1:2 likens the "Spirit-kiss divine" to the moment when God breathed life into Adam. In Jewish history, the "kisses" of God were most often interpreted as moments of divine intervention in the story of his people, for example, their release from Egypt.[14]

Jeanne Guyon, a French Catholic nun who lived from 1648–1717, wrote the following in her commentary on the Song of Songs: "What is this kiss? It is complete spiritual union: a real permanent, and lasting experience of God's nature. The kiss is the union of God's spirit to your spirit."[15]

- *With these interpretations in mind, what prayer would you like to offer now to experience more of God's love in your life?*

- *Begin your own Shulamite journey by praying along with her brave words, "Let him smother me with kisses—his Spirit-kiss divine." Expect a response from God after this prayer.*

WORD WEALTH

The Hebrew word for *kiss* in the text is *nashaq*. Along with the literal or figurative meaning "to kiss," it can also mean "to equip with weapons."[16] In the text, the phrase "I drink them in like the sweetest wine" is a wordplay in the Hebrew between kisses and wine. For example, the baptism of believers with the Holy Spirit in Acts 2 could be considered a kiss from the Beloved. The ultimate equipping of the bride of Christ with his Spirit left them as if they had drunk new wine.

Your Name Is Flowing Oil

• *Read Song of Songs 1:3, including the TPT footnotes for that verse.*

What did the lover's presence release?

To what did the Shulamite compare his name?

According to the footnote, what is another possible translation of "the brides-to-be adore you"?

In both Hebrew and Greek, the name Jesus Christ includes the meaning of *salvation* and *anointing*. In the Hebrew, *Yeshua* means "Adonai saves," and *Hamashiach* means "anointed one." In Greek, *Jesus* means "Jehova is salvation." *Christ* also means "anointed" in Greek and comes from the root word *chrio*, which means "to smear or rub with oil." In Strong's Concordance, the definition includes "enduing Christians with gifts of Holy Spirit."[17]

- *Read Luke 4:18–19 to understand the anointing of Jesus in his own words.*

  What does it mean for the flowing oil of the name and presence of Jesus to continually pour out over your life?

  Have you experienced a time when the power and anointing of Jesus were released when you prayed in his name? Describe what happened.

Draw Me and We Will Run

- *Now read Song of Songs 1:4, including TPT footnotes for this passage.*

  Into where did the Shulamite ask her lover to draw her?

Where did they run together?

According to footnote 'h,' what is the literal text in this verse? What does the "cloud-filled chamber" represent?

What would the Shulamite's friends remember?

Verse 4 is significant to the storyline of the entire book. Most of the song can fall into these two requests: "draw me" and "we will run." The first four chapters of the song will be the drawing of the Shulamite into the heart of the king. The end of the book portrays them running together in union. This model is wonderful to follow in our own spiritual life. So often we can be enticed to run after ministry or destiny without drawing close to God first.

• *What activities in your life help you draw closer to God?*

- *Have you ever prayed for God to draw you closer to himself? Would you consider saying that prayer now?*

- *Pray along with the Shulamite, "Draw me into your heart." Expect a response from God after this prayer.*

 # DIGGING DEEPER

The "chamber within a chamber" or the "cloud-filled chamber" that they run into is a reference to the Holy of Holies. This is the first of several references in the song to the dwelling place, or tabernacle. Solomon, the author of the song, was the builder of the temple in Jerusalem. Solomon's Temple was designed after the dwelling place of Moses that the Israelites moved throughout their forty-year journey in the wilderness.

Scripture's full description of the dwelling place can be found in Exodus 25–30. The Holy of Holies is the inner most chamber of the dwelling place, which held the ark of the covenant. Once a year on the Day of Atonement, the Levitical high priest would offer a goat on the bronze altar. The priest entered the Holy of Holies and sprinkled the blood on the mercy seat of the ark of the covenant to atone for the sins of the nation. A cloud of God's presence rested in the chamber upon the ark of the covenant.

- *Read Matthew 27:50–51. What happened in the temple when Jesus died on the cross? What did this event signify?*

- *Read Hebrews 9:1–10:22.*

   How did Jesus fulfill the role of the old covenant priesthood and the sacrificial system?

   Now, consider the wording in Song of Songs 1:4. What does it mean for the Shulamite to draw close to Jesus and run together into his cloud-filled chamber, the Holy of Holies?

Into the Holy of Holies

As the Shulamite went into the cloud-filled chamber, she immediately experienced her first crisis.

- *Read Song of Songs 1:5, including the TPT footnotes for it.*

  What did she realize about herself in the Holy of Holies?

  How did the Shepherd-King respond?

  As you run into the cloud-filled chamber with Jesus, how do you see yourself? Do you see your shortcomings? Or all that you have done wrong this week? Or do you see the power of his sacrifice in your life, covering you with his holiness? Explain your answer.

  After reading verse 5, how do you believe Jesus sees you?

It is common to be confronted with our own darkness or unworthiness when we see a glimpse of the Bridegroom in the Holy of Holies. We feel covered in sin, but he sees us as a bride who is covered in the blood of his sacrifice. He sees the torn veil and a bride clothed in white robes. One of the most important journeys of the Shulamite is to learn to see yourself through the eyes of your Beloved, covered in the blood of his sacrifice and his holiness.

🔯 WORD WEALTH

In some translations, the entirety of verse 5 is spoken in the voice of the Shulamite, saying, "I am dark, but lovely,...like the tents of Kedar, like the curtains of Solomon" (NKJV). Let's look at the Hebrew to understand why The Passion Translation chose the construction of the Shulamite saying, "I feel as dark and dry as the desert tents of the wandering nomads" and the Shepherd-King responding, "Yet you are so lovely—like the fine linen tapestry hanging in the Holy Place."

According to *The JPS Bible Commentary*, a leading Hebrew resource for understanding the song, the phrasing in the original text can be correctly translated vertically as two parallel pairs, meaning that "I am dark" can be paired with "like the tents of Kedar," and "You are so lovely" can be paired with "like the curtains of Solomon."[18] The context supports this translation because the tents of Kedar would have been dark or blackened. It is also difficult to conceive how the Shulamite would see herself as filled with darkness and lovely at the same time.

This is a significant theme repeating throughout the song. The Shulamite was aware of her imperfections. She was held back by fear because of her insecurities. The Shepherd-King continually encouraged her with his view of her as holy, beautiful, and worthy of love. Over the course of the song, her perspective changes to align with his. As this happens, she steps into the fullness of her identity as the bride and his partner.

💙 SHARE GOD'S HEART

In these first few verses of the song, we meet the friends of the Shulamite. In verse 3, she referred to them as the brides-to-be who adore the Shepherd-King. In the next verse, the friends replied that they will remember the love of the young couple and rejoice and delight in them.

- *Who are the brides-to-be in your life? Who are the people who are watching your journey into a deeper revelation of God's love?*

- *Have they commented on your relationship with God? If so, what have they said?*

- *What can you do to help them see and understand even more of what it's like to be loved by God?*

THE EXTRA MILE

One of the best resources for understanding the Jewish cultural context of the song as well as the nuances in the Hebrew text is *The JPS Bible Commentary: Song of Songs*. In the Jewish tradition, there are four levels of understanding Scripture. The introduction of *The JPS Bible Commentary* explains these at great length. The commentary is structured to show all four levels of interpretation for every passage in the book. This is a particularly helpful way of looking at the Song of Songs because the imagery allows for so many different levels of interpretation. As an example, we will look at Song of Songs 1:3 as interpreted through each level.

Peshat: This is a literal interpretation of the text, focusing on the grammatical meaning of terms and phrases in their given context. It is considered the "outer garment" of interpreting Scripture. An example of the *peshat* in 1:3 is to look at the word *anointing* in the Hebrew and its meaning, which includes "name," "reputation," "fame," and "glory."

Derash: This interpretation considers the wider "communal or religious import" of Scripture. It takes into account how the worldview of the text reflects theological, historical, or ethical matters. An example of *derash* in 1:3 is to describe how God's people throughout the ages have celebrated the name of God.

Remez: This third level of interpretation focuses on the "personal and spiritual value" of Scripture. The *remez* interpretation uses the Scripture as an allegory for your personal spiritual life. An example of *remez* in 1:3 is to describe how the fragrance of God's presence and character come through our life.

Sod: The fourth and most profound level of interpretation is the *Sod*. *Sod* is the mystical interpretation of a passage, uncovering hidden truths deep below the surface. *The JPS Bible Commentary* notes, "As a work believed to be a most special symbolic expression of Scripture, the words of the Song (the holy of holies of Scripture) were read as symbolic prisms of such supernal realities...Thus, reading the Song is a most sacred act, which might enable the adept to ascend the spiritual worlds and conjoin with the divine truths that the text symbolizes." An example of the *Sod* in 1:3 is describing the spiritual experience of praying in God's name and how it transforms natural events with supernatural power.[19]

If this method of study feels significant for you, consider acquiring your own *JPS Bible Commentary on the Song of Songs* and go deeper verse by verse.

Talking It Out

1. What area of your life could benefit from the strategy of "Let him?" Where are you working from your own strength rather than from God's strength? Take time to pray with one another over what your group members share.

2. What interpretation of "kiss me" is the easiest for you to personalize? Share a specific memory where you felt the kiss of God in your circumstances. How did that change the situation and the way you felt about God?

3. When considering the terms "draw me" and "we will run together," which of these phrases best describes your current season with God? Are you in a season of drawing closer together with him? Or are you in a season of running together? Do you feel a need to shift toward one or the other? And how can you make that shift?

4. When you come into the presence of God (the Holy of Holies) during prayer, worship, or meditation, how is your experience similar to or different from the Shulamite's? Are you aware of your sin or darkness? Do you hear the voice of God whispering that you are covered in holiness? How could listening to his voice of encouragement rather than any internal voice of accusation change your quiet times together?

5. What is the most significant personal revelation for you from this lesson? How do you intend to incorporate it into your daily life?

LESSON 3

From Shame to Grace

(1:6–14)

Our Shulamite will have experienced a beautiful breakthrough by the end of this first chapter in the song. She started the story crying out for the return of her first love. She felt lost from her beloved and ashamed of her darkness. By the end of this first chapter, all these issues in her heart will have been addressed. As she listened to her bridegroom's voice of love, her shame was overcome. She came to the King's table of abundance and received the gift of grace. Let's look at the story in more detail.

- *Read Song of Songs 1:6–14 to familiarize yourself with the overall context. What verses or phrases captured your attention? Why?*

My Vineyard Within

- *Read 1:6, including TPT footnote 'e' for this verse.*

    What was the state of the inner vineyard of the Shulamite?

    What was the state of her relationship with her "brothers"?

- *Now read John 15:1–17 and the TPT footnotes for verse 7.*

    What can we learn from verses 4, 7, and 9 of John 15 regarding the tending of our inner vineyard?

    What is our role and what is God's role in tending our inner vineyard?

    What are the visible results of a thriving inner vineyard based on the John 15 passage?

According to verses 12–13 and 17, what is the effect upon our relationships with our fellow cherished friends or "brothers" if we abide in the vine?

• *Read Song of Songs 1:7–8, including the TPT footnotes for these verses.*

What request did the Shulamite make of the Shepherd-King when she realized the state of her inner vineyard?

Can you describe a time in your own life when you felt overwhelmed by your circumstances and cried out to God?

How did he respond?

How did the Shepherd-King respond to the Shulamite in these verses?

The Shulamite began this journey overwhelmed with her own sin and burned out in ministry. She was having some type of contention or disagreement with her brothers in the faith, perhaps over her inability to do enough. She was weary, lost, and wandering. He promised to lead her back to the "sanctuary of my shepherds" (v. 8). This was the gathering of his people, his church. We will find this theme repeated within the song. Whenever she is wandering and lost from him, he encourages her to go back to his sanctuary, his city—his church. This is a significant strategy imparted through the Song of Songs. When you are feeling lost spiritually, return to the gathering of God's people. In the gathering of his people, you will find him again.

🫶 EXPERIENCE GOD'S HEART

Notice the contrast between how the Shulamite saw herself in 1:6 and how her beloved saw her in verse 8. She was filled with shame, yet he called her "radiant."

- *How do you see yourself in the Spirit? Do you see yourself as holy and radiant? Or dark and covered with sin and shame?*

- *John 15:8 exhorts us to continually let his love nourish our hearts. What words of love from this passage in the song can you receive today?*

- *Allow the words of your Bridegroom in these verses to soak into your soul until shame is replaced with his acceptance and love.*

 THE EXTRA MILE

Hudson Taylor (1832–1905) authored his own commentary on the Song of Songs entitled *Union and Communion*. He wrote the following about 1:7–8: "We now come to a very sweet evidence of the reality of the heart-union of the bride with her Lord. She is one with the Good Shepherd: her heart at once goes instinctively forth to the feeding of the flock; but she would tread in the footsteps of Him whom her soul loveth, and would neither labour alone, nor in other companionship than His own."[20]

Union and Communion is a short commentary filled with profound spiritual truths. It is available as a pdf download via internet search. Consider downloading this commentary to further your study of the Song of Songs.

His Healing Words of Encouragement

- *Read Song of Songs 1:9, including the TPT footnotes for this verse.*

  How did the Shepherd-King see the Shulamite?

To what did he compare her?

The healing transformation of the Shulamite began with these words spoken over her, "Let me tell you how I see you." This will be a powerful theme throughout the song. She transformed in response to the words of love he spoke over her. He called her beautiful and strong. Her beauty was in her strength, like a "regal steed pulling [a] royal chariot."

Beautiful Emotions

• *Read verse 10, including the TPT footnotes for this text.*

How did he describe her cheeks?

What do cheeks represent?

In the TPT footnote 'd' for verse 10, the term for *cheeks* is equated to *countenance*. The connotation is that your emotions in all their forms are beautiful to Jesus. Part of the healing journey of the song is learning to express your emotions honestly with Jesus. We are emotional beings, and he created us that way. Emotions in and of themselves are not sin; they are a normal expression of our humanity. Jesus expressed many strong emotions in the Gospels and did so without sinning.

- *What emotions have you been too ashamed of or afraid to share with God?*

- *Take time to pray and share the authentic emotions of your day with God. If this feels difficult, consider the psalms, which often start with David's painful emotions and move to a place of thanksgiving as he remembered the steadfast love of God.*

Adorned with Gold and Silver

- *Read Song of Songs 1:11, including the TPT footnotes for this passage.*

   According to the footnote for verse 11, what does "We" represent?

   With what was the Shulamite adorned at the end of verse 11?

In verse 11, the Bridegroom promised, "We will enhance your beauty, with golden ornaments studded with silver." This is the only time in the song in which the Shepherd-King refers to himself in the plural. As noted in the TPT footnote, some theologians interpret this as the commitment of the Trinity working together to bring the bride into her full beauty.

- *What does gold point to in Scripture (see TPT footnote 'g' for v. 11)?*

- *According to the TPT footnote, what does silver represent in Scripture?*

- *Do any other Scripture verses come to mind with a similar application of gold or silver?*

- *Considering this interpretation of the significance of gold and silver, what does it mean for the Bridegroom to enhance your beauty through these elements?*

Thus, as the TPT footnote suggests, the adorning of the bride through the perfecting of Calvary began her transition from shame to grace.

- *What words or phrases in verses 9–11 feel most significant to you?*

- *Let yourself hear the voice of the Bridegroom speaking of your beauty and worth. Engage him in prayer.*

The King's Table

- *Read verse 12, including the TPT footnotes. For the cultural context of the extravagance of a king's table during the time the song was written, read 1 Kings 4:22–23 and Esther 1:5–8.*

   Based on the passages from 1 Kings and Esther, how would you describe the abundance at the king's table?

   What limits existed upon the guests at the king's table?

- *Now read Psalm 23:5, where the Good Shepherd prepares a table for us, and Esther 7, where Queen Esther prepared a banquet for the king. Considering these two passages, how would you describe the connection between eating at the table with the king and breakthrough in your personal trials?*

- *The second half of Song of Songs 1:12 describes the sweet fragrance of spikenard bursting forth at this banquet. Read the TPT footnote 'f' in 4:13–14 for a better understanding of the significance of spikenard. Then read either Mark 14:1–11 or John 12:1–11 for another story in Scripture where the fragrance of spikenard filled a room.*

> *What was the king doing for the Shulamite in Song of Songs 1:12 when her spikenard fragrances the night?*

> *After reading the meaning of spikenard and the passage of Mary of Bethany in the Gospels, what is the significance of the sweet fragrance of spikenard bursting forth in this moment?*

> *How do you respond when you feel surrounded by the presence of the Bridegroom and are overwhelmed by the abundance of his blessings?*

⚙ THE BACKSTORY

The full meaning of Song of Songs 1:12, sitting at the table and eating together, cannot be truly appreciated without digging a bit deeper into the Hebrew concept of hospitality. First, the Western image of a table and chairs is misleading in the context of the story. This story is written in a Bedouin culture of shepherds. They relaxed and dined in large tents with carpets laid on the ground and cushions surrounding the eating area.[21] Some translations use the word *couch* instead of *table*. Neither term in the Western vocabulary adequately describes the setting of this banquet. The king's table would have been a place of reclining and comfort with an abundance of assorted dishes on the rug in front of them. This is a place of rest and great provision.

It was also a place of peace. "To eat a meal with someone was to be at peace with him (Genesis 26:28–30)."[22]

And finally, the Hebrew culture placed great importance on hospitality. In Zephaniah 1:7, God laid out a banquet for his people and consecrated his guests. Jesus told the parable of a wedding banquet in Matthew 22:1–14, where the invited guests were too busy to come or arrived without wearing their wedding clothes. Failure to appropriately respond to the king's hospitality did not meet with his favor.

A Sachet of Myrrh

- *Read Song of Songs 1:13, including the TPT footnote for it. Also read the TPT footnote regarding myrrh in 4:13–14.*

  How did she describe her lover?

Where was the sachet of myrrh resting?

According to the TPT footnote 'k' in 4:13, what was myrrh known as in Hebrew culture?

According to the TPT footnote for 1:13, what does the bundle of myrrh represent?

• *Read Psalm 45:7–8 and John 19:39–42.*

How did Nicodemus prepare the body of Jesus for burial?

What were the similarities between the spices that Nicodemus used in John 19 and the fragrance of the robes of the Messiah as described in Psalm 45:7–8?

Myrrh plays a prominent role in the song. As we progress, we will see this spice in several key passages. This was the Shulamite's first encounter with myrrh, but she had more challenging experiences to come with this spice. And ultimately, she saw the fullness of its fragrance burst forth in her own life.

- *How can you keep a sachet of myrrh resting over your own heart?*

DIGGING DEEPER

Psalm 45 is titled *The Wedding Song.* According to the TPT footnote for this psalm, some commentators believe it was written about Solomon. Based on this footnote, we will interpret Psalm 45 as a "song of the wedding of Jesus and his bride, the church." We have already seen one cross-reference of the psalm to the Song of Songs.

- *Read Psalm 45, including the TPT footnotes.*

   What verses in the psalm were most significant in the passage for you personally and why?

What verses in the psalm are similar in imagery or meaning to the Song of Songs?

How does Psalm 45 describe the Bridegroom?

How does Psalm 45 describe the bride?

How does this help you understand Jesus better?

How does this help you understand your own role as the bride of Christ? And the role of the church?

Bouquet of Henna Blossoms

- *Read Song of Songs 1:14, including the TPT footnote. Also read the TPT footnote 'e' regarding henna in
4:13–14.*

    According to the footnote, what does the word henna
    mean in Hebrew?

    *Why is it significant that the Shulamite compared the
    Bridegroom to henna?*

    From the footnote, what does "Engedi" mean?

    *Considering the meaning of henna and the vineyard as
    described in John 15, what does "henna plucked near the
    vines at the fountain of the Lamb" mean to you?*

𝕙 WORD WEALTH

The word for *henna* in Hebrew is *kaphar*. In addition to meaning "atonement" or "ransom price," it is also the word for *tar* or *pitch* used in Genesis 6:14–15.[23] Noah covered the ark inside and out with *kaphar*. This is a beautiful picture of the atonement of Christ, who paid the ransom price for our sins. We are covered inside and out with his redeeming grace.

❤ SHARE GOD'S HEART

The Shulamite, as a shepherd girl, led and tended a flock. She continually shared the overflow of her life with those around her.

- *What have you learned about God's love for you in this lesson that you would like to share with friends, family, or those you lead?*

- *Whom would you like to invite to embark upon this Shulamite journey with you?*

- *What opportunities do you have to share this in the upcoming week?*

 THE EXTRA MILE

Are you ready for a challenge? Try using the Jewish model of *Peshat, Derash, Remez*, and *Sod* to interpret a verse from this lesson—a verse from Song of Songs 1:6–14. Here is a reminder of each level of interpretation:

> **Peshat** is a literal interpretation of the text that focuses on the grammatical meaning of terms and phrases in their given context.

> **Derash** interpretation considers the wider "communal or religious import" of Scripture. It takes into account how theological, historical, or ethical matters are reflected in the worldview of the text.

> **Remez**, the third level of interpretation, focuses on the "personal and spiritual value" of Scripture. The *remez* interpretation uses the Scripture as an allegory for your personal spiritual life.

> **Sod** is the deepest level of interpretation. *Sod* is the mystical interpretation of a passage, uncovering hidden truths deep within the passage.

- *What verse did you choose?*

- *What is a Peshat interpretation of that passage?*

- *What is a Derash interpretation of it?*

- *What is a Remez interpretation?*

- *What is a Sod interpretation?*

Try not to be too critical of your attempt at this method. It is a difficult task and takes some thought, prayer, and help from the Holy Spirit.

Talking It Out

1. What have you learned from the Shulamite's journey in this lesson that is helpful to your own?

2. How would you describe your journey from shame to grace?

3. What did you learn about the Good Shepherd in this lesson? What life-giving revelation can you hide in your heart?

4. What spiritual discipline brings you to the King's table of abundance and provision? Where and when in your life are you able to take time to pause in his presence and be reminded of his love and care for you?

5. Our lesson ended with the Shulamite holding a bundle of myrrh over her heart and clutching the henna from the vines at the fountain of the Lamb. What does it mean to hold the sacrifice of Jesus at Calvary and his atoning ransom price so close to your heart daily? During what activities do you tend to lose sight of the victorious sacrifice of Jesus on your behalf? During what activities do you feel the closest union and communion with Christ?

LESSON 4

Resting in His Shady Grace

(1:15–2:7)

The Shulamite began this section with a new understanding of the sacrifice of Calvary and the fullness of the atonement. Shame had been left behind, and she was moving into the wonders of grace. The verses for this lesson will be a journey in learning to rest in his grace and promises.

- *Before beginning the lesson, read Song of Songs 1:15–2:7 to understand the overall context. What verses or phrases seemed significant to you? And why?*

Eyes of Love

• *Read 1:15, including the TPT footnotes.*

> *According to the note, how many times in the song did the Shepherd-King describe the Shulamite as beautiful or most beautiful among women?*

> *What are the other meanings of the word* beauty *in Hebrew?*

> *To what did he compare her eyes?*

> *According to the footnote, what does it mean to have the eyes of a gentle dove?*

• *Read the account of Jesus' baptism in Mark 1:9–11, including the TPT footnotes.*

According to footnote 'c,' what does the dove represent?

What words did the Father speak over Jesus at his baptism that were similar to what the Shepherd-King spoke over the bride in the song?

Our Resting Place

• *Read Song of Songs 1:16, including the TPT footnotes.*

How did the Shulamite describe her beloved in this verse?

How did she describe their resting place?

*Explain the difference between the reality of the
Shulamite in 1:6–7 and verse 16. Where had she arrived?*

Watchman Nee, a Chinese Christian leader who lived from
1903–1972, wrote many works on divine union with Christ, focusing on a genuine experience of the cross. In his commentary on
the Song of Songs, he wrote:

> "Also our bed is green." The maiden has
> attained the rest which she had previously
> sought. There is feeding as well. The grass
> is the bed, and the reclining is the rest.
> This matches Psalm 23:2…The table which
> was mentioned previously also has the
> element of rest, but the emphasis there was
> on eating. Here the bed has an element of
> eating, but the emphasis is on rest…if a
> shepherd is skillful, his sheep will be able to
> lie down even though they are in the green
> pasture. They will have satisfaction and rest.[24]

The first three chapters of the song describe the bridegroom as
the "Shepherd-King." To understand the role of the bridegroom
as her "Shepherd-King," let's read Psalm 23, which describes God as
the Good Shepherd. Take time to carefully read the TPT footnotes
for this psalm as they provide additional context.

- *What parallels can you draw between 1:16–17 in the
  song and Psalm 23:1–3?*

- *What verse in Psalm 23 is ministering to you today in your own walk with Jesus?*

- *When and where in your daily life can you pause and rest in the presence of the Good Shepherd and receive all you need from him?*

Cedar and Cypress

- *Read Song of Songs 1:17, including the TPT footnote.*

   How did she describe the house forming around them?

   According to the footnote, what did Solomon build with cedar and cypress (or pines)?

- *Read 1 Kings 5:4–5.*

   What parallels can you draw between Song of Songs 1:17 and 1 Kings 5:4–5?

   How was rest significant in the building of Solomon's dwelling place?

   How did Solomon describe the impact of the blessing of rest from God in his life?

- *Now read Ephesians 2:20–21 and Hebrews 3:1–5, including the TPT footnotes.*

   According to these passages, what is Jesus building in and through his people?

   As his beloved ones, where must we find our rest?

DIGGING DEEPER

The mention of cedar and cypress in Song of Songs 1:17 is a second reference to the dwelling place in the song. Cedar and cypress were the two primary building materials Solomon used to build his temple in Jerusalem. Throughout the Old Testament, the dwelling place was the physical place where God's presence rested with his people. He gave Moses specific instructions for building the dwelling place in Exodus 25–31. Take a few minutes to review these chapters.

- *What can you observe about the building of the dwelling place from your quick look at these chapters?*

The Israelites camped around the dwelling place in the wilderness.

- *Read Exodus 13:17–22. How does this passage describe God's presence? Did the pillar or the cloud ever leave the Israelites?*

- *Read 2 Samuel 7:1–17, where David spoke of his longing to build a house for God.*

  What was the desire of David's heart in verse 2?

  How did God respond in verses 5–7?

  What did God promise in verses 10–11?

  How do verses 13 and 16 point to the Messiah?

God responded to David's request with a covenant promise. He vowed to "build a house" for his name and "establish the throne of his kingdom forever" (v. 13 NKJV). This was a prophecy of the Messiah coming through the genealogy of David. Hebrews 3:1–5 describes Jesus as a greater builder than Moses because he would establish an eternal house through his people.

The first chapter of the Song of Songs ends with this victorious statement of the bride, describing the rafters and balconies of the house (dwelling place) being constructed over their heads (1:17). According to *The JPS Bible Commentary* on this verse, there is a Jewish tradition of "planting a cedar sapling upon a boy's birth and a cypress upon a girl's, and subsequently using these trees for their bridal bower."[25] In the song, the Shepherd-King and Shulamite are building a spiritual house where they can live together as one. It is the "true heavenly tabernacle" described in Hebrews 8:2. Passages such as this in the Song of Songs are why so many Christian writers throughout the ages have lauded the book as the revelation of union and communion with Christ.

The Rose and the Lily

- *Read Song of Songs 2:1, including the TPT footnote.*

    Who is the rose in the context of this verse?

    Who and where is the lily?

    According to the footnote, what does it mean to be the "rose of Sharon"?

    What is the song that the Shepherd-King sang over the Shulamite?

    What is an alternate definition for the word rose *in this verse?*

- *Another verse in the Bible that speaks of "overshadowing" is Acts 5:15, the account where people are healed in the shadow of Peter. Read this verse, including the TPT footnote.*

    According to the footnote, what is the word episkiazo *used for exclusively?*

    According to the footnote, what other verses or stories in Scripture use this term "overshadow"?

Take note of the transformation of the Shulamite at the beginning of Song of Songs chapter two compared to the beginning of chapter one. She now saw herself as the one he sings over. Her reality was no longer "I am dark." His words of "You are lovely" took root in her heart. Her self-judgment was diminishing in response to his words of love. Shame was gone.

- *Read Song of Songs 2:2, including the TPT footnotes.*

    How did the Shepherd-King describe her?

    According to footnote 'g,' what do the thorns represent in this verse?

    How did he describe her purity?

A "lily among thorns" is one who is living in the revelation of grace but is still surrounded by sin in her life. The ultimate goal of the bridegroom was to get her to the top of a mountain where she would reign in victory. Her position in this chapter showed a growing work of grace in her life, but she had not overcome the valley of sin.

The Apple Tree

• *Read 2:3, including the TPT footnote.*

> *Who was compared to an apple tree in this verse?*

> *What happened to the Shulamite as she sat under his grace-shadow?*

> *What did she eat?*

> *Where did she rest?*

- *According to the footnote, the phrase "sons of men" in this verse can also be translated as "trees of the forest." Read the following verses and note how trees can represent humanity.*

Mark 8:24

Psalm 1:1–3

Jeremiah 17:7–8

Isaiah 55:12–13

 DIGGING DEEPER

Many commentaries relate the imagery of Jesus as a tree like no other tree in the forest to the Tree of Life in Genesis 2. Father Arintero (1860–1928) wrote in his commentary, "Thinking of Christ as the precious Apple Tree or as the Tree of Life, as opposed to the other apple tree in which she found death, the soul sees Him hanging from the holy Tree of the Cross and there she sits to slowly contemplate the ineffable mysteries of a love stronger than death itself that moved Him in this way to sacrifice Himself for us so as to give us life."[26]

Resting under the shade of this "holy Tree" is to rest in the grace of the cross, where his glory never fades. To rest in the shade of his grace is to stop trying to earn our own righteousness and fully rest in the righteousness of Christ.

The House of Wine

• *Read Song of Songs 2:4, including the TPT footnote.*

> *As she rested under the shade of his grace, where did he transport her?*

> *What did she experience there?*

> *How did he look at her?*

> *According to the footnote, what banner did the Shulamite live under?*

In Acts 2:1–13, when the disciples experienced the baptism of the Holy Spirit, onlookers commented that the believers had been drunk on new wine. Brian and Candice Simmons write, "For the believer, the house of wine is that place of experiencing the Holy Spirit."[27]

Overcome with Love

• *Read Song of Songs 2:5–6, including the TPT footnotes.*

What happened to the Shulamite in the house of wine?

What did she eat?

According to the footnote, what is the significance of raisin cakes in verse 5?

According to the footnote, what do the apples or apricots represent?

What was the Shulamite longing for?

Where did she rest?

How would you describe the heart and spirit of the Shulamite at this point in the story?

The Shulamite fainted in the arms of her beloved, overcome with the power of his love for her. They rested together in a lover's embrace. He cradled her close, supporting her head.

Do Not Disturb Love

• *Read verse 7, including the TPT footnote.*

What did the Shepherd-King say to the friends of the Shulamite while she was passed out in his arms?

According to the footnote, what do the deer and gazelles represent?

Some commentators will take this verse out of context by warning believers not to fall in love too quickly. The context of the verse clearly shows that the Shulamite was overwhelmed by love and rested in the Shepherd-King's embrace. He encouraged those around her to let her linger there as long as she desired. This was not a caution against divine love. It was a caution to leave her alone in this moment with her beloved until she was ready to arise.

This exhortation not to disturb or awaken love occurs several times in the song. Each time, the context is similar. The Shulamite was so overwhelmed with his love that she became incapacitated. Each time, the bridegroom warned the others not to awaken her from this state until she was ready.

EXPERIENCE GOD'S HEART

The Song of Songs describes a beautiful journey of maturing in faith. As believers, we will experience every season described in the song. In the season of a lily among the thorns, we are holding tight to the sacrifice of Christ but still living among the thorns. The first couple of chapters give the strategies for moving beyond this reality. First, listen to his words of love over your life and let that drown out the self-talk of shame. Second, find your rest inside his shady grace. Dive deep into grace and receive it right where you are. Often, we try to clean ourselves up so we can come back into his presence. The lesson of the Song of Songs is to invite the Bridegroom into the reality that we are living and allow him to transform it. As we continue reading, we will see that he gets her out of this valley of thorns. And it wasn't through her hard work. It was through her ability to rest in him. Let him do his work for you.

- *In what area in your life do you still struggle with the reality of sin as you cling to the Beloved?*

- *Pause for a time of reflection and allow the voice of the Bridegroom to speak into your heart the truth of his love for you. Allow his voice to quiet the voice of condemnation that likes to arise inside. As you rest in the power of his grace, let shame lift away from you.*

- *Take time to journal what you feel the Lord is speaking into your heart during this time.*

❤ SHARE GOD'S HEART

This lesson has been an invitation to rest in the grace of God. Leave the overwhelming pace of life for a few moments and pause in his presence. Listen to his beautiful voice and let the transforming power of his love seep into your soul.

- *Who in your life would be blessed most right now by a few moments of rest and connection? Think of someone who rarely takes time for themselves but is always doing something for others. Invite them to coffee or a meal together and pass along to them the blessing you have received from this lesson. Share with them that they are loved, valued, and appreciated. Let the love of God that you have received shine through for them.*

⬆ THE EXTRA MILE

We have just completed one chapter in the song, and already we have found two references to the dwelling place. We have several more references coming in the song. If you are not familiar with the dwelling place of Moses, consider doing some additional research to understand its significance in the Old Testament to the Jewish people and its significance in the New Testament for

Christian believers. The heart of the Song of Songs is union and communion with God. The dwelling place is the symbolic representation of God dwelling with man in union and communion. This is an in-depth study, but for those who choose to complete it, the revelatory blessing will be profound.

Most people find a pictorial diagram of the dwelling place helpful while studying the different sections and furniture. You can easily find these on the internet, along with descriptions of the significance of the individual parts.

Scripture passages to study:

- *Exodus 25–31: The dwelling place of Moses*
- *2 Samuel 7: God's covenant with David*
- *1 Chronicles 15–17: David's dwelling place*
- *1 Chronicles 21:18–22:19: David's organization of the dwelling place supplies and instruction for its construction*
- *2 Chronicles 2–7: Solomon's Temple*
- *Ephesians 2:20–22: God's dwelling place*
- *1 Peter 2:5: Living stones*
- *Hebrews 3–10: The true tent*

Talking It Out

1. What have you learned from the Shulamite's journey in this lesson that is helpful to your own?

2. What are practical ways you can rest in the shade of the grace of Jesus in your everyday life?

3. How can you invite others into that same rest? Did you try the "Share God's Heart" activity in this lesson? If so, share your experiences and then pray together for those with whom you shared God's love.

4. What is the role of the Holy Spirit in experiencing the fullness of the love of Jesus? Share a story of a time when the Holy Spirit made God's love real for you.

5. Have you ever been transported to the house of wine with God? Describe your experience. Pray together for everyone in the group to experience a greater measure of the Holy Spirit in their lives.

LESSON 5

The Invitation

(2:8–17)

In the opening verses of chapter two, the Shepherd-King has brought the Shulamite to a safe harbor of rest and grace. In the house of wine, he overwhelmed her with the fullness of his love for her. She was lost in love; however, she was still in the valley among the thorns. She had silenced the voice of shame inside herself and was receiving his words over her life.

As we will see in the next section, she had not reached the fullness of all the Shepherd-King had for her. Would she be able to overcome the fear that held her back and accept his invitation?

- *Before beginning the lesson, read Song of Songs 2:8–17 to understand the overall context. What verses or phrases stand out to you? Why?*

Leaping over Mountains

• *Read verses 8–9, including the TPT footnotes.*

  How did the Shulamite know the Bridegroom was coming to her?

  In what form was he coming to her?

  What was he leaping over to get to her?

  Where was she hiding?

  In these verses, who was removing the separation between them—the Shulamite or the Shepherd-King?

Brian and Candice Simmons wrote in their commentary:

> The gazelle is swift and sure-footed,
> walking on high places. This is a new
> revelation of Jesus to the bride. The
> inscription of Psalm 22 reads, "For the
> Pure and Shining One – David's song of
> anguish to the tune of 'The Deer at the
> Dawning of the Day.'" This speaks of
> Christ's resurrection. Jesus is the deer who
> leaped out of the dark tomb on resurrection
> morning; He skips in resurrection power.
> The maiden begins to recognize His
> strength and agility to overcome every
> obstacle. He is coming to bid her to arise
> and go with Him in that same power.
> Jesus loves you so much that He will climb
> mountains just to be with you, even a
> mountain called Calvary. This truly is love.[28]

DIGGING DEEPER

Psalm 22 is a prophetic song that foretells the coming Messiah and his sacrifice on Calvary. There were thirty-three prophesies in this psalm fulfilled by Jesus on the cross. The Jesus of Calvary—he is the one who will leap over every mountain of separation between you and his presence. Sin (the valley of thorns) separates us from God, but Jesus' blood reconciles us to God.

- *Read Psalm 22, including the TPT footnotes for a more in-depth understanding of the text.*

  What is the significance of the wording in verse one (compare it to Matthew 27:45–46)?

What verses can you identify as pointing to the coming Messiah?

What is the similarity between the last verse of the psalm and Jesus' experience on the cross?

How does Jesus leap over the mountains of separation to his bride?

What walls have you created in your life that can make it seem that God is far off?

How can a deeper understanding of the cross and Jesus as the deer at the day's dawn remove this feeling of separation?

🄷 WORD WEALTH

Psalm 22 ends with the declaration, "It is finished!" These are also the final words of Jesus on the cross. The phrase is written in Greek in our Gospel accounts, but most scholars agree that Jesus likely spoke this sentence in Aramaic, his heart language. The Hebrew and Aramaic words are the same in this instance. There is an interesting hidden meaning within this expression, as explained in the TPT footnote for John 19:30:

> This is from the Hebrew word *kalah*, which has a homonym that means "fulfilled [completed]" and "bride." Jesus finished the work of our salvation for his bride. This translation has combined both concepts. For a fascinating study of the Hebrew word used for "bride" and "finished," with its universe of meaning, see *Strong's Concordance*, Hb. 3615, 3616, 3617, 3618 and 3634. Although the completed work of salvation was finished on the cross, he continues to work through his church today to extend God's kingdom realm on the earth and glorify the Father through us. He continues to work in us to accomplish all that his cross and resurrection have purchased for us, his bride. His cross fulfilled and finished the prophecies of the Messiah's first coming to the earth. There was nothing written that was not fulfilled and now offered to his bride.[29]

The Shulamite's name also holds a similar revelation. The word for her name in Hebrew is *sulamiyt*, which means "the perfect" or "the peaceful." It comes from the root word *salam*, which has a number of meanings, including "completed," "finished," "perfect," "restored," and "restitution."[30] The meaning of the phrase "It is finished!" is included in the very name of our shepherd girl who will be restored by her Shepherd-King.

- *Read John 19:28–37, including the TPT footnotes. Meditate on the profound mystery in the final act of Jesus Christ in this passage.*

Come Away with Me

- *Read Song of Songs 2:10, including the TPT footnotes.*

  What was the invitation of the Shepherd-King to the Shulamite in this verse?

  How does this verse answer her prayer in 1:4?

  According to footnote 'j,' how does the word arise *point to the ark?*

According to footnote 'k,' what does the word darling *mean in Hebrew?*

How does your spirit respond to the Bridegroom Jesus calling you his dearest, his complete one, his beautiful one?

- *Read Matthew 11:28–30, including the TPT footnotes.*

  What do we find when we answer the call to come to Jesus?

  According to footnote 'i' for verse 29, what does the yoke point toward?

  According to verse 29, what do we find when we come to Christ?

• *Read Psalm 55:22–23.*

   Where are we to leave our cares and worries?

   What will strengthen us?

   Whom does he watch over?

   Where is our hope and trust?

Signs of a Changing Season

• *Read Song of Songs 2:11–13, including the TPT footnotes.*

   *The description of seasons in these verses begins
   and ends with the word* change. *Describe the change
   that the Shepherd-King called forth from within the
   Shulamite.*

What does the winter season represent in verse 11?

According to footnote 'a,' what does the rain represent?

According to footnote 'b,' what do the flowers point to?

According to footnote 'c,' what is another translation for "singing" in Hebrew?

According to footnote 'd,' what does the turtle dove represent?

According to footnote 'e,' what does the fig tree represent?

If the vine represents the bride, what do "budding vines…blooming everywhere" represent?

In verse 13, the Shepherd-King gave a second invitation to the Shulamite to come away with him. To where did he invite her?

We can learn many lessons by observing the changing seasons in a vineyard. Sometimes, as believers, we expect to produce a continual harvest. In the annual cycle of the seasons, we see that each one has a purpose. The shift from one season to the next provides a natural rhythm of rest and nourishment for the vines. The dormant winter season is often a time of rest and pruning. Although this season may feel unproductive, there will be no new vintage of wine without it. Spring brings with it the possibility of new beginnings. The summer season is a time of growth and expansion. Fall is a time of harvest and gathering to share in our abundance.

What season are you currently experiencing?

Have you experienced pruning in your life? How did it create the opportunity for new beginnings?

What are the new seeds being planted and watered in your life?

What will the harvest of this season yield?

Take time to pray for each season to produce its purpose in your life.

 # THE EXTRA MILE

In their commentary *The Sacred Journey*, Brian and Candice Simmons describe this section about the changing seasons as "eight prophetic signs of the new life He is calling her to. A spiritual springtime has now come. He's sharing these secrets with her so that she will arise and come with Him. These words are meant to assure her of His power and of the approaching harvest. These eight statements are meant to stir her heart to arise and come away, for the season has changed and now it is time to experience resurrection life."[31]

- *Study the Simmons's description of these eight changes of seasons and what they mean for a believer on pages 83–87 in their commentary. Then identify which of these seasonal changes (if any) the Lord is currently calling you toward.*

Hidden in the Split-Open Rock

- *Read Song of Songs 2:14, including the TPT footnotes.*

  Where was the Shulamite hidden?

  According to footnote 'f,' what does the cleft of the rock represent?

  Who put her there?

  What was she doing there?

 EXPERIENCE GOD'S HEART

Many commentaries compare this verse to the story in Exodus 33, when God hid Moses in the cleft of a rock and passed before him with his goodness. This is symbolic of being hidden in the pierced side of Christ, where we are sheltered from the judgment of God and instead graced with his glory.

- *Read the following Scripture verses (including the TPT footnotes). Journal how each one describes Christ as a Rock.*

  Psalm 118:22; Matthew 21:42; Acts 4:11

  Isaiah 8:14; Romans 9:33

  Isaiah 28:16

  1 Corinthians 10:4

  1 Peter 2:4–8

- *Read Exodus 33:18–22 and John 19:33–34, including the TPT footnotes.*

What did you learn about the heart of God in these passages?

In your daily thoughts, do you have a mindset of being judged by God or being the one for whom he would give his life to save from judgment?

Pause in a quiet moment and see yourself placed gently into the cleft of the Rock, the pierced side of Jesus, where he shelters you from God's wrath and instead shows you his goodness.

Journal what it means to be hidden in the life of Christ.

 WORD WEALTH

In Song of Songs 2:14, the Shepherd-King hid the Shulamite in "the secret stairway of the sky." Through the death and resurrection of Jesus, we are seated in a heavenly place with him.

• *Read Colossians 3:1–4 and Ephesians 2:4–6, including the TPT footnotes.*

> *What do these verses reveal about where we are seated with Christ?*

> *As you go about your daily activities, do you experience the reality of being seated with Christ, or is this something you can lose sight of?*

> *Pause in a quiet moment and see yourself being placed in the secret stairway of the sky, seated with Jesus in a heavenly place. What does your spirit experience as you meditate on this reality?*

> *These are wonderful verses to hide within our hearts. One way to more deeply take in Scripture is to memorize it. As we memorize a passage, it affects how we view ourselves and the world around us. Commit Colossians 3:3 and Ephesians 2:6 to memory. Repeat them aloud daily until these verses are firmly planted within your spirit.*

Catching the Foxes

In Song of Songs 2:14, the Shepherd-King spoke so many beautiful encouragements over the Shulamite: she was his dove, she was radiant, her voice was sweet. She was beautiful in her place of worship and intercession. And yet these encouragements were not enough for her to overcome her fear and come away with him. Knowing that she was not going to come with him, the Shepherd-King brought the focus back to her garden within.

• *Read 2:15, including the TPT footnote.*

> *What were the foxes doing to the Shulamite's vineyard?*

> *According to the footnote, what do foxes represent in our lives?*

> *Who caught the foxes in this verse?*

> *Pause for a moment and pray. Ask the Holy Spirit to show you the foxes that are causing damage to your vineyard. Ask for his help to remove them. Then journal what God revealed to you during your prayer.*

Held Back by Fear

• *Read verses 16–17, including the TPT footnotes.*

> *What did the Shulamite say before she responded to the Shepherd-King's invitation?*

> *How would you describe her confidence in his love in this moment?*

> *How did the Shulamite respond to his invitation to come away with him?*

> *What was her excuse for not going with him?*

> *According to footnote 'b,' what do the mountains represent?*

The first part of verse 16 is sometimes translated, "My beloved is mine, and I am his." Just before she declined his invitation, the Shulamite revealed her revelation of grace. Even though she ultimately failed the test at this moment, this verse shows a profound change in her understanding of his love. She knew that he would not stop loving her, even if she turned him down. This wording will appear again later in the song, in a place where she fully aligned her will with his. The difference in context between the two instances is noteworthy.

Afraid of the Dark

The Shulamite was held back from following her beloved because of her fear of the darkness. She said, "until the day springs to life and the shifting shadows of fear disappear." How often can we as believers allow our fear of the darkness that confronts us to hold us back? This wording will echo again in chapter four of the song, during the Shulamite's greatest moment of breakthrough. She wasn't quite mature enough in her relationship with the Bridegroom to conquer her fear at this moment, but victory was coming. This verse is the introduction of an important theme in the song. The Shulamite feared the dark in this moment, but she ultimately brought the light.

• *Has fear ever held you back from what God has called you to do? Of what were you afraid?*

• *Were you able to grasp the grace of God, who still loves you? What did that do for you?*

Mountain of Spices

We learn in Song of Songs 2:17 that the Shepherd-King invited the Shulamite to the "mountain of spices." In 4:6, it will be referred to as the "mountain of suffering love" or the "mountain of myrrh" (see TPT footnote 'd'). We studied the significance of myrrh in 1:13 and discovered that myrrh represents the sacrificial death of Christ. In the Song of Songs, the "mountain of myrrh" is Calvary. The Shepherd-King invited the Shulamite to come with him to Calvary. She wasn't ready yet and encouraged him to turn and ascend the holy mountain without her.

 SHARE GOD'S HEART

The heart of Jesus of Calvary shines through in chapter two of the Song of Songs.

- *Invite a few friends to study Psalm 22 together. Share with them what you learned about the King who leaps over mountains of separation.*

Talking It Out

1. What have you learned from the Shulamite's journey in this lesson that is helpful to your own?

2. Do you feel God is calling you into a new season? If so, what is his invitation? How have you responded? Stop and pray for one another as the need arises in this discussion.

3. What have you learned about God's grace in this lesson?

4. What foxes do you need to catch for the promises of God to fully take root? Pray with each other that you can fully remove these hidden compromises from your lives.

5. Song of Songs 2:14 reveals how much your worship and intercession please God. Share together what you are thankful for this week. Praise God's name for the blessings he has given you and pray for one another to experience more of his love.

LESSON 6

Lessons from the Night Season

(3:1–11)

Chapter three of the song starts a new scene in this epic play. Our Shulamite had some time to live with her decision to send her beloved ahead without her, and it wasn't sitting well. This section of the story begins with her in the depths of despair. Despite being rejected, the Shepherd-King will lift her up from these circumstances and set her back on the path of her destiny. Thus far in the song, the Shepherd-King has not referred to the Shulamite as the "bride." These are still the days before their covenant union.

- *Before beginning the lesson, read Song of Songs 3:1–11 to understand the overall context. What verses or phrases stood out to you? And why?*

The Dark Night

- *Reread verses 1–2, including the TPT footnote.*

  Was this dark night of the soul just one night for the Shulamite or many?

  Where did she look for the Shepherd-King?

- *Read Matthew 5:14, Isaiah 26:1–2, and Revelation 21:2. Taking these verses into consideration, what does the city represent in 3:2 of the song?*

- *Read Song of Songs 3:3–4, including the TPT footnote.*

  Who helped the Shulamite find the one her soul loved?

How did the overseers in verse 4 guide her to her beloved?

Who are the spiritual leaders in your life who can point you toward Jesus and then step out of the way?

What did the Shulamite do when she found her beloved?

To where did she bring him back?

• *Read verse 5. How does the context of 3:5 compare to 2:7?*

The Shulamite began by feeling overwhelmed with depression, regret, and loneliness. She searched the city for her Shepherd-King and was quickly reunited with her beloved. This pattern of going back to the church or the gathering of believers repeats in the song. It occurred in chapter one, and it will happen again in chapter five.

When you are feeling spiritually lost or alone, return to a gathering of God's people, a church group where you experienced his presence before.

The reader can easily identify the godly overseers because they immediately pointed her directly to her beloved. They didn't set themselves up as an in-between, and they didn't abuse her for her failures.

Just as she moved past the overseers, she found the one her heart adored. She was caught up again in his embrace and went back to the place of union with him, into the temple, the Holy of Holies. Again, in this moment of holy embrace, the Shepherd-King implored the Jerusalem maidens by everything that is pure and innocent not to disturb them. This is the second time these words appear in the song, and again they are in the context of a lover's embrace.

The Merchant Bridegroom

• *Read Song of Songs 3:6, including the TPT footnote.*

Who was speaking in this verse?

What does a pillar of glory cloud ascending from the wilderness point to in Scripture? See Exodus 13:21.

Recall what myrrh represents in the song and summarize that here.

According to the footnote for Song of Songs 3:6, what does frankincense represent?

Who did the Shepherd-King say is more fragrant than these spices?

• *Read Matthew 13:44–45, including the TPT footnotes.*

According to the footnote, who is the merchant in this parable?

What does the field represent?

Who is the treasure?

What price did the person pay to purchase the field?

- *Read Isaiah 43:4, 1 Corinthians 6:19–20, and Ephesians 5:25–27.*

  What was the price that Christ paid for his bride?

  According to the Ephesians passage, why did Christ die for us?

Now, reread Song of Songs 3:6 and consider the symbolism of this One arising from the wilderness, fragrant with myrrh and frankincense, more fragrant than a merchant. This is a beautiful picture of Jesus of Calvary, arising from the grave, where he paid the ransom price for his bride and presented her to himself as holy and pure.

 DIGGING DEEPER

Let's pause for a moment from the Song of Songs story and look at another passage of Scripture that describes the relationship between God and his people as a bridegroom and his bride. Isaiah 54 describes God's tender love for Zion.

- *Read Isaiah 54, including the TPT footnotes.*

  What similarities do you see between the bride described in Isaiah 54 and the Shulamite?

What differences do you see between them?

According to the TPT footnote for verse 1, how is spiritual barrenness broken?

How is God described in verse 5?

In what way does Isaiah 54:8 parallel the Shulamite journey?

What did God promise to his bride in Isaiah 54:10?

What did God promise to his bride in verses 11–13?

What did God promise to his bride in verse 17?

The Bride's Carriage

• *Read Song of Songs 3:7–10, including the TPT footnote.*

> *What arrived to transport the Shulamite to the wedding (v. 7)?*

> *What surrounded the carriage (v. 7)?*

> *How were the sixty champions equipped, and what was their purpose (vv. 7–8)?*

> *Who made the mercy seat (v. 9) and the carriage (v. 10)?*

> *What rested or dwelled above the carriage (v. 10)?*

What was their seat sprinkled with (v. 10)?

What covered the carriage (v. 10)?

 WORD WEALTH

The Hebrew word for "marriage carriage" in 3:7 is *mita*, which means couch, bed, or bier (which is a frame to carry a coffin).[32] In various translations, it is called a litter, couch, or palanquin. This term describes a couch or bed on a pole frame on which the bride reclines as tenants carry her to the wedding. This type of special transport for a bride is still used in Eastern weddings today. For a visual, type the word *palanquin* into a search engine and view the images.

As described by Brian and Candice Simmons in their commentary:

> The Holy Spirit wants to show us the
> King's glorious nuptial carriage. This is the
> wedding carriage, or palanquin, carried on
> the shoulders of His servants. In ancient
> times, far eastern brides were carried
> on men's shoulders in a sedan chair,
> referred to as a carriage. The bride and
> groom reclined within the veil, screened
> by curtains from public view. Bodyguards
> accompanied them as blazing torches lit
> up their pathway. This is the picture the

Lord would show us of how we are carried through life in His covenant grace. We dwell with Him behind curtains. Like the Ark of the Covenant, we are hidden with Him, concealed from the world and carried throughout life.[33]

The Ark of the Covenant

The description of the marriage carriage in Song of Songs 3:7–10 has several parallels to the ark of the covenant that was placed in the dwelling place of Moses.

- *Read Exodus 40. What parallels do you notice between Song of Songs 3:7–10 and the dwelling place constructed under Moses?*

- *Read Exodus 13:21–22. What does the pillar of the glory cloud in the wilderness represent?*

- *Read Exodus 25:10–16. How does the marriage carriage resemble the ark of the covenant?*

- *Read Exodus 25:17–21 and Leviticus 16.*

    What is the symbolism of the bride sitting on the "mercy seat"?

    What does the sprinkle of crimson on the mercy seat represent in 3:10 of the song?

- *Now, reread Song of Songs 3:7–10.*

    What are the implications of the marriage carriage carrying you to Calvary?

    How can you learn to rest more fully in the life and death of Jesus, as the Shulamite rested upon the palanquin?

Paved with Love

In his sermon entitled "Paved with Love," Charles Spurgeon used the King James Version translation of 3:10, "The midst thereof being paved with love, for the daughters of Jerusalem." Spurgeon went on to share an interesting insight into the making of the palanquin. He discussed different interpretations of this wording, one being that the bottom of the palanquin was paved with precious stones. He felt that was unlikely and shared another possible interpretation: "Therefore, others have explained the passage as referring to choice embroidery, and dainty carpets, woven with cost and care, with which the interior of the travelling-chair was lined. Into such embroidery sentences of love-poetry may have been worked...tokens of love were carved or embroidered, as the case may have been, upon the interior of the chariot, so that 'the midst thereof was paved with love.'"[34]

The Wedding Procession

- *Read Song of Songs 3:11.*

    Where were the Shepherd-King and the Shulamite headed in this carriage?

    How did the voice of the Lord describe this day?

    Whom were the brides-to-be watching?

♥ EXPERIENCE GOD'S HEART

At the end of chapter two, fear held the Shulamite back, and she encouraged the Shepherd-King to go on without her. In the opening of chapter three, we saw the depth of her regret in that decision. In many ways, this chapter is a transition between her failure and her victory. She will have a chance to confront the same obstacles in chapter four and make a better choice. Sometimes as believers, we can sink under a wave of condemnation when we make a mistake in our spiritual walk. One of the healing themes of the song is the bridegroom's embrace of the Shulamite despite her mistakes.

Instead of condemning the Shulamite for her poor choices, the Shepherd-King embraced her and held her as long as she needed. Then he showed her a better way, the way of Calvary. The very darkness that she was afraid to confront lost its power when the marriage carriage picked her up. Chapter three is a good reminder that we can make it much further in his strength than in our own.

- *Take a quiet time of reflection and consider the following questions:*

  What moments in your spiritual walk with God do you regret or wish you could have another opportunity to make a different choice?

  Were you trying to walk in your own strength rather than in God's grace during those times?

In a time of prayer, ask God for his forgiveness and ask for his grace and strength to carry you in these kinds of situations in the future.

Allow the Bridegroom Jesus to embrace you and lead you to the marriage carriage in the Spirit. Receive the heart of the Merchant King, who laid down his life to cover your sins. Sit upon the mercy seat sprinkled with his blood and allow him to heal the pain and regret from this experience. Then journal what God revealed to you during this time with him.

❤ SHARE GOD'S HEART

In the last verse of chapter three, the voice of the Lord invited the Zion maidens or brides-to-be to celebrate the wedding procession of the King. This procession brings into focus Jesus of Calvary, who paid a price to restore his bride to holiness. The Song of Songs creates an opportunity to share the story of the cross embedded deeply in a context of love. Rather than just covering our sin, the purpose of Christ's sacrifice was to restore us to union with God. It brings a new dimension to the call of evangelism in our lives.

- *Who are the Zion maidens in your life? Who are the ones who seem interested in hearing about the love of God that you have experienced?*

- *Try sharing your testimony of faith with one of these brides-to-be. Share how God's love has touched you personally and made your life better. Share what you have learned about God's love for you and them.*

- *If the opportunity arises, share the story of the cross and how Jesus sacrificed his life to cover your sins. And then ask if they would like to experience the same love of God in their own lives. If they are not a believer, invite them to receive Jesus as their personal Savior.*

- *If they agree, pray with them to receive Jesus as their Savior. Invite them to study the Bible or go to church together.*

 THE EXTRA MILE

In this lesson, we experienced the true heart of the Bridegroom Jesus. A brief study into Jewish wedding customs can add an even deeper level of understanding of his heart for the bride. Try typing "how Jesus fulfilled Jewish wedding customs" into an internet search engine and read some of the articles or Bible study helps that appear. This may provide a new understanding of some Gospel accounts where Jesus subtly refers to the wedding customs.

Talking It Out

1. What have you learned from the Shulamite's journey in this lesson that is helpful to your own? Share your journeys with one another.

2. What did you learn from the Shulamite's night season that could help you in the future when you feel like you let down God?

3. What did you learn about the power of grace and the fullness of Christ's sacrifice in your life? How might that help you in your relationships with fellow brothers and sisters in Christ?

4. In the arrival of the marriage carriage, we see an invitation for the bride to rest in Christ's work on the cross. In what area of your life have you been operating in your own strength rather than allowing Christ to transport you through? What would it look like to invite him into your struggle and rest in him?

5. What was your level of understanding of the dwelling place of Moses and the ark of the covenant before this lesson? Did questions or thoughts arise as you studied some of this Old Testament imagery? Share your questions and thoughts with one another. Study more deeply, if need be, to find the answers together.

6. When you consider relating to Jesus as your Bridegroom, does that feel awkward? Or as you study the song, is it becoming more of a reality? Share your experiences of learning to relate to Jesus in this new way. Pray with one another as the Spirit leads.

LESSON 7

Fear Overcome

(4:1–8)

As we came to the end of chapter three in the song, our lovers were being carried on the palanquin, heading to their wedding. By the halfway point of chapter four, the Bridegroom-King will call the Shulamite his "bride" for the first time. The section of Scripture we will cover in this lesson, 4:1–8, sits between their arrival to their nuptials and the declaration of her now being the bride. Thus, this section is the wedding ceremony. This is the Shulamite's pivotal experience of entering into divine union and covenant with the bridegroom.

- *Before beginning the lesson, read chapter four of the song to understand the overall context. What verses or phrases stood out to you? Why?*

A Flock of Goats

• *Read 4:1, including the TPT footnote.*

> *How did the Bridegroom-King describe the Shulamite in the opening sentence?*

> *What did he see when he looked into her eyes?*

> *According to the footnote for verse 1, what does "a flock of goats streaming down Mount Gilead" represent?*

> *What is the meaning of comparing her hair to this flock of goats? What did he see in her?*

Brian and Candice Simmons write the following about this verse:

> When the King notices her heart yielded
> in holy devotion, it moves Him. Her long
> hair is compared to a flock of goats that
> have descended from Mount Gilead. Gilead
> was the place where the sheep and goats
> were kept, awaiting sacrifice in the temple.
> The sacrificial lambs grazed on Mount
> Gilead. Jesus extols the bride's dedication,
> comparing it to a goat coming from the

mountain ready for sacrifice. She becomes a "*living sacrifice*" by her response to the mercies of God (Rom. 12:1).[35]

In these mysterious words, "like a flock of goats streaming down Mount Gilead," some of the deepest revelation in the Song of Songs is hidden. This is why so many of the martyrs quoted verses from the Song of Songs during their moment of persecution. This text describes the dedication that would bring someone to offer their very life as a sacrifice for Christ.

In this verse, the Bridegroom saw within the Shulamite her readiness to offer her life as a sacrifice (which she will do in 4:6). To be clear, the sacrifice she offered here was not to earn her own salvation. Her salvation was secured much earlier in the song, in the first few chapters. Rather, she was taking up her cross and following him. The ultimate expression of union with Christ is allowing your life to be a sacrifice with his. For most, this will not mean losing their physical life for the sake of the gospel; however, persecution or loss for his sake can come in many different forms and experiences.

Rahab's Scarlet Ribbon

• *Read Song of Songs 4:2–3, including the TPT footnotes.*

What did the Shulamite eat at the king's table that was displayed in her life now?

How did the Bridegroom-King describe her in verse 2?

According to footnote 'b' for verse 3, what is the signifi-cance of her lips being like Rahab's scarlet ribbon?

According to footnote 'c,' what does it represent to com-pare her cheeks to a pomegranate?

How does the pomegranate represent the temple and the priesthood?

The Promised Land

Throughout the song, we will see several references to the promised land. This was the land God promised to his people Israel when he rescued them from slavery in Egypt. By the time of King Solomon and the writing of the Song of Songs, the Israelites had been living in their promised land for several generations. King Solomon would have heard the stories of the journey of his ancestors many times. He used imagery related to the promised land repeatedly in the writing of the song. He pointed specifically to Rahab in two verses. Let's dig a bit deeper into this history in Scripture to better understand this divine poetry.

• *Read Matthew 1:1–6.*

  How was King Solomon related to Rahab?

  How was Rahab related to Jesus?

• *Read Numbers 13:1–14:24 and Hebrews 3:7–19.*

  According to Numbers 13:23, what were the fruits of the promised land?

  Why were the Israelites who spied out the land in Numbers 13 unable to enter the land in the same generation?

  According to Hebrews 3, what was the sin of the Israelites?

• *Read Joshua 2, including the TPT footnotes.*

> *Describe Rahab's role in the opening of the promised land for the Israelites.*

> *What was the significance of the crimson rope?*

> *How did Rahab's actions in this story differ from those who initially spied out the land in Numbers 13 and were not allowed to enter?*

• *Now reread Song of Songs 4:3–4.*

> *What does the king see on the cheeks (or countenance) of the Shulamite?*

> *How does her union with him in this moment compare to the Israelites entering into their land of promise?*

This is one of several instances in the song that will connect the Shulamite's mouth with the promised land. Her mouth represents her expressions of love and devotion. Her cheeks reveal the love on her countenance. In the next few verses, her words will open the promised land for the Bridegroom to conquer, like Rahab's red rope did for the Israelites. The Shulamite's journey progresses from eating the Bridegroom's promises under the apple tree in chapter two to opening up the promised land in chapter four to living with him in the promised land in chapter eight. She was a shepherd girl looking for the ultimate place to pasture her sheep. The pasture that he led her to is the land of promise, his eternal kingdom.

David's Fortress

- *Read Song of Songs 4:4–5.*

  How did the Bridegroom-King describe the Shulamite's strength?

  What was the enemy's response?

  How did the Shulamite provide for the next generation?

🅗 WORD WEALTH

The wording of the first half of verse 4 in Hebrew is literally "your neck is like a tower of David." The Bridegroom-King praised the Shulamite's neck three times in the song (1:10; 4:4; 7:4). In the first instance, her neck was adorned with jewels. In the second and third, he compared her neck to David's tower and an ivory tower. Initially the Bridegroom described her neck as beautiful. In chapter four, he highlighted her strength. In chapter seven, he extolls her purity.

The neck in Scripture often represents the will of man. In 2 Chronicles 30:8, God warned the Israelites against having a stiff neck, which is an unwillingness to yield to him. He didn't allow them to enter their land of promise because of their hardened hearts (Hebrews 3 and Psalm 95). The progression of the description of the Shulamite's neck in the song relates to her yielding her heart to the Bridegroom. As we grow and mature, as we yield our will to the Lord's, we grow in strength and purity.

David's tower was the place where the weapons of war were stored. The Bridegroom-King saw his betrothed with a will as strong and equipped as the tower of David, yielding to his will. She could withstand the enemy's attack, and ten thousand soldiers would surrender to her beauty.

The Bride's Vow

• *Read Song of Songs 4:6, including the TPT footnotes.*

How is 4:6 similar to 2:17?

How is 4:6 different from 2:17?

In 4:6, where did the Shulamite commit to go with the Bridegroom-King?

What did the Bridegroom-King call the Shulamite at the end of verse 6?

Verse 6 starts with "I've made up my mind." Of her free will, the Shulamite decided to follow him now. She made this choice in the darkness before dawn, with a nearly identical parallel to 2:17. This time she made a different choice. She said yes to going with him to the mountain of myrrh and the hill of burning incense. The scene had not changed between the two verses; it was still dark outside. We are still waiting for the dawn to arise, but this time she overcame her fear of the unknown, her fear of the dark, her fear of whatever the mountain may hold. She said yes. She yielded her will to his.

Song of Songs 4:6 is the hinge of the book. This verse represents the wedding or agreement of covenant union between the couple. He called her "bride" for the first time. From this point forward in the story, she truly began walking in her destiny as his partner. The Shulamite journey before this verse was radically different than after this verse.

Take Up Your Cross

• *Read Matthew 16:24–27, including the TPT footnotes.*

What did Jesus ask of his disciples?

What did Jesus promise in return?

• *Read Galatians 2:19–21.*

   What is the outcome of being crucified with Christ?

   Taking this passage into account, what should we see in the Shulamite's life after Song of Songs 4:6 when she decided to climb the mountain of myrrh with him?

• *Read Philippians 3:9–11.*

   From where does our righteousness come?

   How are we able to experience "complete oneness with him"?

The Mountain Top

• *Read Song of Songs 4:7–8, including the TPT footnotes.*

How did the Bridegroom-King describe the Shulamite's beauty in this moment?

Where did he take her?

According to footnote 'c,' what does "the crest of Amana" represent?

According to footnote 'd,' what did the newlyweds gaze upon from their mountaintop?

The Bridegroom-King called his bride "perfect" in this passage. This was the first time he used this word to describe the Shulamite in the song. He praised her perfect beauty in the context of her yielding her will to him, in her willingness to take up her cross and follow him to the mountain of suffering love.

As they went together to the mountain of myrrh (Calvary), she entered the realm of faith. She was seated with him in a heavenly place, in "a place of settled security." In this realm of faith, she will realize God's promises (see Ephesians 2:6 and Colossians 3:1).

 EXPERIENCE GOD'S HEART

Preachers often liken reading the Song of Songs to reading a love letter from God to his people. Sometimes as we study the Shulamite's journey, we can forget to receive the healing words in these passages for ourselves. As you read the following paraphrased expressions of God's love for you, pause and linger on each one. Allow yourself to internalize the truth of his love for you, his bride. Internalize his acceptance of you and his delight in you. Try not to disqualify yourself from his love because of your thoughts about not being good enough. One of the greatest lessons of the Song of Songs is learning to receive the love and acceptance of Jesus despite our own shortcomings.

- *Pause and reflect upon each statement, journaling anything the Holy Spirit reveals to your heart.*

> *When I look at you, I see my perfect creation. I call you "good." I see your beauty.*

> *I see the Spirit of God active and working within you as I gaze into your eyes.*

> *As I look into your heart, I see your gentleness and your purity.*

I am overwhelmed by your devoted worship and sacrifice for my name.

You have eaten from the abundance of my Word, and your life is producing the fruit of the promised land.

Your words of grace and mercy open my promises in your life and to those around you.

I enjoy experiencing all your genuine emotions. Your authenticity delights me.

The beauty of your surrender to me causes those who fight against us to lay down their weapons.

Faith and love exude from within you and touch those around you.

Every part of you is beautiful to me, my darling.

♥ SHARE GOD'S HEART

In this section of the song, we found two passages that lend themselves to sharing God's heart with those around us. The first is in 4:3 where the Bridegroom-King described the gracious and mercy-filled words of the Shulamite's mouth as being "refreshing as an oasis." The second is in 4:5, where the Shulamite nurtured the "infants" or those new to their faith.

- *Write a list of those you know who are new in their faith journey. Commit to spending time with one or more of them in the next few weeks.*

- *During your time together, share how much God loves and accepts them, no matter where they are in their journey. And share how you have experienced God's love yourself. Pray with them for a greater understanding of God's love and grace in their lives.*

✪ DIGGING DEEPER

One way to understand Scripture more fully is to study the life of someone who embodied that message. Madame Jeanne Guyon was a Catholic mystic who lived and preached life-union with her beloved Jesus. Jeanne Guyon was born on the eve of Easter, 1648, in Montargis, France, about fifty miles from Paris. She spent portions of her early childhood in a convent. At the age of sixteen, she entered an arranged marriage with a thirty-eight-year-old man. The union was an unhappy one. They had five children, of whom only three survived into adulthood. At the age of twenty-eight, Madame Guyon became a widow.

Madame Guyon then dedicated her life to the devotion of Christ. She had several mystical experiences with the love of God. She wrote about one of these experiences: "I felt at this instant deeply wounded with the love of God;—a wound so delightful, that I desired it never might be healed." And, "Oh Beauty, ancient and new! Why have I known thee so late? Alas, I sought thee where thou wast not, and did not seek thee where thou wast! It was for want of understanding these words of thy Gospel: '*The kingdom of God cometh not with observation, neither shall they say, Lo! Here, or lo! there; for, behold, the kingdom of God is within you.*' This I now experienced, since thou didst become my King, and my heart thy kingdom, where thou dost reign a Sovereign, and dost all thy will."[36]

Madame Guyon wrote prolifically about the love of Christ in manuscripts, poetry, and letters to friends. Her most read work is *Experiencing the Depths of Jesus Christ,* which is considered a Christian classic. She wrote a commentary on the Song of Songs, which was one of the first interpretations of the song as a personal journey with God. *Union with God*, a collection of her poems and letters, makes a wonderful devotional.

During her lifetime, the Catholic church was still contending with the effects of the Protestant Reformation. Jeanne Guyon was imprisoned several times for expressing a grace theology and encouraging believers to experience life-union with the beloved Bridegroom.

After publishing *A Short and Very Easy Method of Prayer*, Guyon was put on trial by the Catholic Church. Her arbiter was Archbishop Bossuet, who was called "The Catholic Church's answer to Martin Luther." Bossuet requested further manuscripts for review from Guyon. She had just completed her Song of Songs commentary and submitted it to him. The priest was scandalized by its intimate language of love.[37] She was imprisoned at Vincennes, a convent at Vaugirard, and the Bastille. She spent the final years of her life living with her children, continuing to write about the love of the Bridegroom. She remained devoted to the Catholic Church until her death at age sixty-nine.[38] Her written works have continued to impact countless followers of Christ for centuries.

Talking It Out

1. What have you learned from the Shulamite's journey in this lesson that is helpful to your own?

2. As we progress through this journey, are you growing in your ability to receive words of admiration and praise from God? How would you describe your ability to receive his love without brushing it off or feeling unworthy?

3. In what area of your life do you feel God inviting you to a place of greater sacrifice or surrender? Are you ready to make that sacrifice?

4. After studying this section of Scripture, how would you describe the value of your yes to Jesus? What does it mean to him and for your experience of life-union moving forward?

LESSON 8

The Garden Restored

(4:9–5:1)

The second half of chapter four of the song and the beginning of chapter five include some of the most vivid, beautiful descriptions of the bride of Christ coming into her glory. This section poignantly portrays the love of the Bridegroom Jesus for his bride. We should read it with both the corporate church and our individual experience in mind. Our Shulamite had overcome her shame and her fear. She was no longer a tired, shepherd girl whose own garden had been neglected. We can now enjoy the transformation of her garden through the eyes of the King.

- *Before beginning the lesson, read Song of Songs 4:9–5:1 to understand the overall context. What verses or phrases stood out to you? Why?*

His Captured Heart

- *Read 4:9, including the TPT footnotes.*

   What impact did her gaze of love have upon him?

   What are the three "names" that he called her in the beginning of the verse?

   According to footnote 'e,' what is another translation for "equal"?

   According to footnote 'f,' what does the Hebrew word libabethini mean in this context?

 WORD WEALTH

One of the more confusing words in most translations occurs in 4:9. The Passion Translation uses "equal" while many other translations use the word "sister." The word in Hebrew is *ahot.* *Ahot* is an irregular feminine form of *ah*, which means "a brother" in either a physical or metaphorical sense. The latter would indicate "someone of equal standing or resemblance."[39]

In many cultures, when communicating with someone who is of equal standing to oneself, you may call them your brother or sister, even though you are not biologically related. In the context of this verse, it would be quite awkward for the Bridegroom-King to call his bride by the title *sister* unless he is using the term metaphorically. Nothing in the context of the song would support the Shulamite being the biological sister of the king. Thus, the translator's choice of the word "equal" instead.

Even understanding this reasoning, how do we process the concept of being "equal" with Christ? The meaning of this wording is perhaps better applied in the context of being seated with Christ in a heavenly place. By joining with the bride in covenant union and becoming one with her, he has raised her up to sit beside him. The King raised the Shulamite to rule and reign beside him.

- *Read Romans 8:17, including the TPT footnotes.*

  What is the outcome of being joined with Christ?

  How are we co-glorified with him?

  How does this verse relate to the Bridegroom-King's invitation to the Shulamite to go to the mountain of myrrh with him?

Honeycomb, Milk, and Honey

• *Read Song of Songs 4:10–11, including the TPT footnotes.*

> *How did the Bridegroom-King describe what the Shulamite's love feels like to him?*

> *What effect did her words of praise have upon him?*

> *According to footnote 'a,' what is the symbolism of milk and honey in her words?*

> *How did the Bridegroom describe the Shulamite's worship?*

Once again, we see a comparison to the promised land. This time it is related to the Shulamite's words of love and worship. Her tongue released milk and honey. Her words were like the sweetest honeycomb to him. The fragrance of her worship surrounded them.

• *Read Ephesians 1:11 and Psalm 110:7.*

> *What do these verses teach us about the connection between union and inheritance?*

A Private Garden and Secret Fountain

· *Read Song of Songs 4:12.*

> *How many times had the Bridegroom-King called her his bride in this chapter?*

> *How did the Bridegroom-King describe his bride in verse 12?*

> *How did he describe their connection?*

> *What did it mean to be his perfect partner?*

THE BACKSTORY

In 4:12, the Bridegroom-King described his bride as "a secret spring" and "my bubbling fountain" that is hidden away from the world. In their commentary, Brian and Candice Simmon wrote:

> There is a legend that King Solomon had a secret sealed fountain known only to him. He had it sealed in such a way that only with his signet ring could it be opened and the water able to flow. The doors of the secret spring would open up, releasing sweet waters of which no one could drink except him. We have become Jesus's holy sacred fountain, sealed by the Holy Spirit (Eph. 4:30). Every Christian should feel that he or she has God's seal upon them. We should be able to say with Paul, "From henceforth let no man trouble me, for I bear in my body the marks of the Lord Jesus" (Gal. 6:17, NASB).[40]

Psalm 110:7 says, "Yet he himself will drink from his inheritance as from a flowing brook; refreshed by love he will stand victorious!"

Isaiah 58:11 says, "YAHWEH will always guide you where to go and what to do. He will fill you with refreshment even when you are in a dry, difficult place. He will continually restore strength to you, so you will flourish like a well-watered garden and like an ever-flowing, trustworthy spring of blessing."

- *What did God promise about the garden and the spring of his people in this verse?*

Her Restored Garden

- *Read Song of Songs 4:13–14, including the TPT footnotes.*

   What do pomegranates symbolize in her garden? (See TPT footnote 'd' for verses 13–14 and footnote 'c' for verse 3.)

   Recall what henna symbolizes and summarize that here. (See TPT footnote 'e' for 4:13–14 and 'k' for 1:14.)

   What does spikenard symbolize? (See TPT footnote 'f' for 4:13–14 and 'i' for 1:12.)

   What does saffron symbolize? (See TPT footnote 'g' for 4:13–14.)

   What does calamus symbolize? (See TPT footnote 'h' for verses 13–14.)

   What does cinnamon symbolize? (See TPT footnote 'i' for verses 13–14.)

Recall what myrrh symbolizes and summarize that here. (See TPT footnote 'k' for verses 13–14 and 'e' for 3:6.)

What do aloes symbolize? (See TPT footnote 'l' for 4:13–14.)

• *Read Song of Songs 1:6, 12–14, and 2:11–13.*

> *How does the inner garden of the Shulamite in 4:13–14 compare to 1:6?*

> *What was different about the myrrh and henna between 1:13–14 and 4:13–14 (hint: external vs. internal)?*

> *How did the Shulamite's inner garden in 4:13–14 now reflect the words the Bridegroom spoke over her in 2:11–13?*

◔ DIGGING DEEPER

These spices are used in many other Scriptures outside of the Song of Songs. Here is a synopsis of where else they are found in the Bible.

Pomegranate: The hems of the priestly robes were decorated with pomegranates made of blue, purple, and scarlet yarn in Exodus 28:33 and 39:24–25. Pomegranates were one of the identifying fruits of the promised land in Numbers 13:23 and Deuteronomy 8:8. The columns in the temple of Solomon were decorated with sculptures of pomegranates in 2 Kings 25:17, 2 Chronicles 3:16 and 4:13, and Jeremiah 52:22–23.

Henna: Henna is not mentioned in Scripture outside of the Song of Songs.

Spikenard: Spikenard is mentioned in only one other biblical event. In the Gospel of Mark, Mary of Bethany anointed the head of Jesus with spikenard just before the crucifixion. In the Gospel of John, she anoints his feet in the same event. Jesus likely smelled of this costly oil as he was crucified. (See Mark 14:3 and John 12:3.)

Saffron: Saffron is not mentioned in Scripture outside of the Song of Songs.

Calamus: The Hebrew word for *calamus* appears frequently in Old Testament stories as a reed. It is part of Pharoah's dream that Joseph interpreted in Genesis 41. It is used to describe the branches of the golden lampstand in the dwelling place in Exodus 25 and 37. Calamus is also part of the sacred oil used in the dwelling place in Exodus 30:23.

Cinnamon: Cinnamon appears in a few Scripture passages. It is one of the ingredients of the sacred oil used in the dwelling place in Exodus 30:23. It also appears in Revelation 18:13.

Myrrh: A caravan of myrrh carried Joseph away to Egypt in Genesis 37:25. Myrrh appears again in Joseph's story in Genesis 43:11. It is one of the ingredients of the sacred oil used in the dwelling place in Exodus 30:23. First Kings 10:25 and 2 Chronicles 9:24 describe the leaders of nations bringing myrrh to Solomon to hear his wisdom. In Esther 2:12, oil of myrrh was part of the six-month beauty treatment for the young women in King Ahasuerus' harem. In Psalm 45:8, the coming Messiah is described with robes fragrant with myrrh. In Matthew 2:11, myrrh is one of the gifts the wise men brought to Jesus at his birth. Christ was offered wine mixed with myrrh at the crucifixion in Mark 15:23. In John 19:39, Nicodemus brought myrrh and aloes to anoint the body of Jesus. Myrrh is also mentioned in Revelation 18:13.

Aloes: In Balaam's third oracle in Numbers 24:6, he uses planted aloes to describe the blessing of the Lord for his people. In Psalm 45:8, the coming Messiah is described with robes fragrant with aloes. Nicodemus brings myrrh and aloes to anoint the body of Jesus in John 19:39.

- *Which of these instances of the spices in other Scripture passages gave you a further understanding of the Shulamite's fragrant garden?*

 # EXPERIENCE GOD'S HEART

Let's pause for a moment before moving to the next verse in the song. The verses we have studied so far in this lesson share beautiful encouragements from the heart of the Bridegroom-King for his bride. Read each of the following paraphrased declarations from Song of Songs 4:7–14, taking time to pause and reflect on each one. Journal anything God reveals to your heart as you meditate on his words of love.

- *Every part of you is perfect. You are without flaw (v. 7).*

- *You are ready to enter the archway of faith with me (v. 8).*

- *You have stolen my heart with your worship. I am held hostage by your love (v. 9).*

- *Righteousness and grace shine upon you (v. 9).*

- *Your love is my finest wine (v. 10).*

- *Your loving words are like the honeycomb to me (v. 11).*

- *I receive my inheritance from the promised land flowing within you (v. 11).*

- *Your priestly intercession arises like a fragrant offering to me (v. 11).*

- *The fruit of mercy is maturing within you (vv. 13–14).*

- *You are releasing my light to the world around you (vv. 13–14).*

- *You have poured out your costly lover's perfume for all to see (vv. 13–14).*

- *My redemption rises as a sweet fragrance from your life (vv. 13–14).*

- *You are holy (vv. 13–14).*

- *You have come to the mountain of suffering love with me. You are covered in my death and resurrection (vv. 13–14).*

- *The balm of healing flows from your life (vv. 13–14).*

A Well of Living Water

- *Read Song of Songs 4:15, including the TPT footnotes.*

   What was flowing from the Shulamite's fountain?

What was springing from within her?

• *Read John 7:37–39, including the TPT footnotes.*

> *What did Jesus promise would flow from the innermost being of those who believe in him?*

> *What did Jesus say the living water represents?*

• *Read John 4:5–30, including the TPT footnotes.*

> *What did Jesus offer the Samaritan woman (v. 10)?*

> *What did Jesus promise to the Samaritan woman (v. 13)?*

> *What would the drink of water become in her life (v. 14)?*

According to the footnote for verse 30, what was this woman's name, and what was her significance in Christian history?

What do Photini and the Shulamite have in common?

 # SHARE GOD'S HEART

A beautiful part of the Shulamite's journey was her transformation from a dry, spiritual desert to a fountain of living water. Sometimes in life we can find ourselves in a season where we desperately need refreshment.

- *Recall a time when life felt like a spiritual desert or when you felt like you had been wandering in a wilderness. How did God minister to you in that season?*

- *Who were the believers in your life that brought you refreshing drinks of grace?*

- *Is someone close to you currently going through a difficult time? Ask God to reveal to you how you can be a source of refreshment for them. Reach out to them and share what is in your heart.*

A Call to the Spirit

- *Read Song of Songs 4:16, including the TPT footnotes.*

    According to footnote 'a,' what does the north wind represent? And what does the south wind represent?

    Why did the Shulamite want these winds of the Spirit to blow upon her garden?

    What invitation did she make to her beloved at the end of the verse?

Why did she now refer to her garden as "your" paradise garden?

Eden Restored

• *Read Song of Songs 5:1, including the TPT footnote.*

According to the opening line of this verse, where was the garden?

Write down the "my" statements in this verse (for example, "my equal").

What had the Bridegroom-King gathered from his garden?

Whom did the Bridegroom-King invite to enjoy the feast in his garden?

Was the garden still locked or enclosed by the end of this verse?

The heart of the Shulamite had now become the garden of Eden restored for the heavenly Bridegroom. He was gathering the sacred spices and enjoying the wine of his Spirit. He was receiving the full reward of his ransom price for his bride. He was partaking of his inheritance, the fruit of his promised land within her. Her life was producing the fruits of his Spirit, and he offered it as a feast to the nations. He encouraged them to "drink and drink, and drink again…Drink the wine of her love." What did he offer the nations? The revelation of Love.

Talking It Out

1. What have you learned from the Shulamite's journey in this lesson that is helpful to your own?

2. What have you learned about God's perspective of your holiness and perfection in him through this lesson? Are you able to receive this truth in your life?

3. How have you processed the statement "my equal, my bride" from the verses in this lesson? Do you perceive yourself as seated with Christ in a heavenly place on a day-to-day basis? Why or why not?

4. This chapter in the song describes a restored Eden through the bride of Christ. Have you ever considered this a spiritual reality that you could experience on earth through Christ? Or have you thought of it as something that you will experience in heaven after this life? How has the study in this chapter impacted your thoughts on this topic?

5. At the end of chapter four, the Shulamite invited the winds of the Spirit to blow in her life to make her garden more fragrant for the king. Have you ever prayed for the winds of the Spirit to blow through your life? If so, what was the result of that prayer?

LESSON 9

The Fellowship of His Suffering

(5:2–16)

Our last lesson finished with the bridegroom and the bride delighting together in their restored garden. The bride called for the winds of the Spirit to make her garden more fragrant. The events in the next chapter in the song are a response to that prayer. The winds of testing and trial will come into her life, followed by the winds of restoration. She will go to the mountain of myrrh and the mountain of incense to experience suffering love. Some may find this portion of the song difficult to read; however, it contains rich lessons for believers. For those who have experienced painful encounters with their brothers and sisters of faith, this lesson offers a unique perspective on how to respond in those moments.

- *Before beginning the lesson, read Song of Songs 5:2–16 to understand the overall context. What verses or phrases stood out to you? Why?*

The Gethsemane Man

• *Read Song of Songs 5:2, including the TPT footnote.*

> *What was the Shulamite doing at the beginning of this passage?*

> *Of whom did she dream?*

> *What did the Bridegroom-King ask of her?*

> *How did he describe her in this verse?*

> *How did he describe himself?*

> *According to the footnote, what does the literal Hebrew text mean? And what does it represent?*

The Intercession of Jesus

To better understand the bridegroom's invitation to the bride in verse 2, let's read the Gospel story of Jesus in the garden of Gethsemane.

- *Read Matthew 26:36–46, including the TPT footnotes.*

  According to the footnote for verse 36, what does Gethsemane *mean?*

  What similarities do you see between the disciples in this passage and the Shulamite in Song of Songs 5:2?

- *Read John 17:1–18:1.*

  What portions of this prayer stand out to you as you read it? Take note of them here.

  What is significant about the heart of the "Gethsemane" Jesus?

When the "Gethsemane Man" invited the Shulamite to arise from her slumber and join him, what was he inviting her into?

The Sleepy Bride

- *Read Song of Songs 5:3–6, including the TPT footnote for verse 3.*

    What held the Shulamite back from joining her Bridegroom-King?

    How did he stir her heart in this moment?

    What was the fragrance upon him? What did it represent?

    What happened when she finally opened the door of her heart to him?

What did she commit to do at the end of verse 6?

Our Shulamite was initially caught up in her own comfort and did not respond immediately to the Bridegroom's invitation to join him in intercession. She quickly regretted this as the fragrance of his suffering melted her heart. By the time she agreed to join him, he had left without her. Thus begins the portion of the story where the Shulamite enters the fellowship of his sufferings.

Suffering and Glory

In preparation for what is coming in the Shulamite story, let's look at another passage in the Bible that addresses how Christians should respond to suffering.

• *Read 1 Peter 4:12–19, including the TPT footnotes.*

> *Why can we rejoice when we share in the sufferings of Christ?*

> *Should we be surprised when we experience tests or trials?*

> *According to verse 14, what is the great blessing that comes with being insulted for Christ's name?*

In verse 19, what does Peter encourage us to do when we suffer for following God's will?

Lost and Abused

Moving back to the song, let's continue with the story of the Shulamite.

- *Read Song of Songs 5:7–8, including the TPT footnote.*

    Where did the Shulamite go to look for her Bridegroom? What did the city represent? (See the footnote for 3:2.)

    Who did she encounter there?

    How did they treat her compared to the treatment of the overseers in 3:2–3?

    What did she say to the brides-to-be in this moment?

In *The Sweetest Song*, pastor Richard Wurmbrand wrote about this verse:

> The watchmen of the city represent the pastors of the Church. Instead of helping the bride to find her Beloved, they beat her and wound her and take away her veil. Jesus foresaw that some of his pastors would begin to persecute his servants. They would care only about eating and drinking and enjoying themselves. In olden times many great persecutions against believers were unleashed by priests who, under the pretext of defending the Church, mistreated the children of God who were meek and spiritual.[41]

 DIGGING DEEPER

Richard Wurmbrand was a Lutheran pastor in Romania of Jewish descent. In 1948, he began preaching against the communist government in his country, declaring the atheist regime to be in conflict with Christianity. He was imprisoned and tortured for fourteen years for his bold sharing of the gospel. He spent over three years of that time in solitary confinement, where he preached sermons to himself each night. He was briefly released from prison from 1956 to 1959, and he immediately resumed ministering through the underground church. In 1959, he was arrested again and sentenced to twenty-five years imprisonment.

The physical torture he experienced during his imprisonment was extreme. He was beaten on the bottoms of his feet until the flesh was gone from the bone, only to have the beating repeated the next day. His captors burned him, cut him, and locked him in a refrigerator cell with almost no clothing. He said that words could not describe the pain. In the midst of his persecution, Richard never lost his love for the Bridegroom.

His supporters ultimately paid a ransom of $10,000 for his release in 1964, after which he left the country to live in Norway. Richard eventually made his way to England and the United States. He shared the stories of his torture before the US Congress, taking off his shirt to show the scars.

Richard Wurmbrand and his wife, Nicolai Ionescu, founded *Voice of the Martyrs* in 1967. He became known as "The Voice of the Underground Church." In addition to his commentary on the Song of Songs entitled *The Sweetest Song*, Richard also wrote eighteen books. His most famous work was *Tortured for Christ*, in which he shared the stories of those who had been tortured by communist regimes.

It is hard to imagine someone who had a greater understanding than Richard Wurmbrand of the revelation in chapter five of the Song of Songs. He went through unimaginable persecution and yet continued to share God's love and the hope of the gospel for the rest of his days. He passed away in Torrence, California, in 2001 at the age of ninety-one.[42]

What Love Is This

• *Read Song of Songs 5:9.*

What surprised the Jerusalem maidens in this verse?

What did they see in the bride because of her response during her persecution?

One of the greatest questions in life asks, *If God is good, why do bad things happen?* This is especially difficult when the bad things happen at the hands of those you trust. Let's see how the Shulamite responds to the question of the maidens.

Radiant and Ruddy

• *Read verse 10.*

> *What was the Shulamite's first response to the maidens about her beloved?*

> *How did she describe his divinity?*

> *How did she describe him in relation to other men?*

 # WORD WEALTH

In Song of Songs 5:10, the Shulamite began a long description of her Bridegroom-King with his divinity and humanity. The bride used two contrasting words to describe her beloved. The first in Hebrew is *sah*, which means "radiant," "dazzling," "glowing," or "bright." The second in Hebrew is *adom*, which means "red" or "ruddy." *Adom* comes from the root word *adam*, which means "to show blood," "red," or "ruddy."[43]

The TPT footnote for Genesis 1:26 says, "According to the Talmud, the three Hebrew letters of Adam's name represent the initials of three men: Adam, David, and Messiah. The Hebrew word '*adam* means 'to show (blood) red,' and *adamu* means 'to make.' The statement to 'make (*adamu*) Adam (ruddy) from (red) soil (*adamah*)' is full of Hebrew puns that are lost in translation."[44]

• *Read Hebrews 1:3, including the TPT footnotes.*

   How was the divinity of God reflected in Jesus?

   What did Jesus accomplish regarding sin?

   Where was Jesus seated?

• *Read Colossians 1:15–17 and 2:9.*

   How do these verses describe the radiant glory of Jesus?

What exists through him?

What finds completion in him?

The Shulamite's beloved is radiant and ruddy. He is the Son of God and the Son of Man.

Ten-Fold Description of the Bridegroom

In *The Sacred Journey*, Brian and Candice Simmons describe the next section of the song:

> What follows is a magnificent tenfold description of the Bridegroom. She is now gazing at Him and worshipping Him in the beauty of holiness. She will use the metaphors of the physical body to convey the virtues and glory of the Man Christ Jesus. This is the Ancient of Days, the Creator of heaven and earth. Here are some features about the life and leadership of our King.[45]

Here is the ten-fold description of the Bridegroom Jesus Christ as categorized by the Simmons:[46]

1. Sovereign leadership (Song of Songs 5:11)

2. Holy dedication (v. 11)

3. Loving insights (v. 12)

4. Exquisite emotions (v. 13)

5. Life-giving words (v. 13)

6. Perfect power (v. 14)

7. Tender compassion (v. 14)

8. Ways of wisdom (v. 15)

9. Excellency (v. 15)

10. Tender love (v. 16)

We will study 5:11–16 through these topical headings. Many of the cross-referenced verses in these sections are suggested in *The Sacred Journey*. For a deeper study of this section of verses, read the Simmons' full commentary for these verses in *The Sacred Journey*.[47]

Sovereign Leadership

• *Read Song of Songs 5:11.*

How did the Shulamite describe her beloved's leadership in this verse?

What did he wear upon his head?

• *Read Colossians 1:18 and 2:10, including the TPT footnotes for these verses. What do these verses reveal about Christ's leadership?*

- *Read Ephesians 1:20–22, including the TPT footnotes.*

  Where was Christ placed when he was raised from the dead?

  What do these verses reveal about his leadership?

- *Read Revelation 19:12, including the TPT footnotes.*

  How does this verse describe the Messiah?

  According to footnote 'b' for verse 12, what do his crowns represent?

Holy Dedication

- *Read Song of Songs 5:11, including the TPT footnote.*

  What was written upon the Bridegroom's crown?

According to the footnote, what is the poetic significance of his locks of black, wavy hair?

• *Read Hebrews 13:8 and James 1:17, including the TPT footnotes. What do these verses reveal about Jesus?*

• *What do these passages—Psalms 102:26–28 and 103:17—reveal about our security in him?*

• *Read Revelation 1:17–18. What does this verse reveal about his holy authority?*

Loving Insights

- *Read Song of Songs 5:12.*

    How did the Bridegroom-King see everything?

    Where did his eyes rest?

    When you imagine Christ looking at you, do you believe he sees your faults or your holiness or both?

- *Read Colossians 1:20–22, including the TPT footnotes.*

    To what has Christ restored you (v. 20)?

    How does he see you (vv. 21–22)?

Exquisite Emotions

- *Read Song of Songs 5:13, including the TPT footnotes.*

    What did the Shulamite see in her beloved's face?

    To what did she compare his emotions?

- *The Gospels are full of stories where Jesus shows a myriad of emotions: joy, sadness, exhaustion, empathy, compassion, and even anger. What are your favorite stories in Scripture that show the emotions of Jesus?*

Life-Giving Words

- *Read Song of Songs 5:13.*

    How did the Shulamite describe the words of her beloved?

Recalling the meaning of myrrh, what would you say is the symbolism of the phrase "lilies dripping with myrrh"? (Hint: look back at 2:1–2 for the use of lily.)

• *Read John 6:63. What are the words of Christ to us?*

• *Read John 7:46 and Luke 4:22. How do these Scripture verses describe the words of Jesus?*

• *Read Psalm 45:2. How does "The Wedding Song" describe the words of the Bridegroom Jesus?*

- *Read John 6:47, 68–69. (Read John 6:22–69 if you are unfamiliar with the story.)*

  What is the living truth that Jesus speaks?

  How did Peter describe the words of Jesus?

Perfect Power

- *Read Song of Songs 5:14.*

  What did the Bridegroom-King's hands hold?

  How did he always use his power? How did he never use it?

- *Read Luke 5:17 and Acts 10:38. How did Jesus walk in perfect power?*

- *Read Ephesians 1:19–21. How do we experience his power?*

- *Read 2 Peter 1:3–4. What does this passage reveal about his divine power?*

Tender Compassion

- *Read Song of Songs 5:14.*

  How did the Shulamite describe her beloved's innermost place?

  In what was he covered?

Concerning this verse, Brian and Candice Simmons wrote in their commentary, "'His innermost place' can also be translated 'His belly' or 'His yearning heart.' The use of this particular Hebrew word conveys the meaning of tender compassion, a yearning heart."[48]

Read Jeremiah 31:20. The footnote in The Passion Translation says, "'Or my inward parts [emotions] rumble.' It is hard to imagine a more tender, loving passage of Scripture than v. 20. God's love for those who fail him is in focus here."[49]

- *What does this verse in Jeremiah reveal about the tender compassion of God?*

Ways of Wisdom

- *Read Song of Songs 5:15. How did the Shulamite describe the Bridegroom's "ways" in this verse?*

- *How did Jesus grow in wisdom as a boy (Luke 2:40, 52)?*

- *How did people respond when Jesus taught in the synagogue (Matthew 13:54–56)?*

- *How do we receive the wisdom of Christ (1 Corinthians 1:30)?*

- *What is Christ the Lamb worthy to receive (Revelation 5:12)?*

Excellency

- *Read Song of Songs 5:16. How does the Shulamite compare him to other men?*

The wording in this verse is similar to 5:10, which says he "stands above all others" and is "outstanding among ten thousand."

- *Read Colossians 1:15–18. What does this passage reveal about the supremacy of Christ?*

- *Read 2 Corinthians 4:6. What do we see when we gaze into the face of Jesus Christ?*

- *Read Revelation 5:5–14.*

    Who is the only one found worthy?

    What phrases in these verses light within you the fire of worship for Christ?

Tender Love

- *Read Song of Songs 5:16.*

    How did the Shulamite describe the Bridegroom's love in this verse?

    Why did she love him so?

    In the last sentence, she called him by what two names?

- *Read Romans 5:8. How did Christ prove his love for us?*

- *Read Ephesians 5:22–32, specifically in the context of Christ and his bride.*

    How does this passage describe the leadership of Christ for his bride?

What is the outward act of his tender devotion to his bride?

How does this passage describe the union of Christ and his bride?

❤ EXPERIENCE GOD'S HEART

Now that we have taken a deeper look at the attributes of Christ listed in chapter five of the song, we can next take time to make a personal connection with the Beloved Bridegroom.

• *Read Song of Songs 5:10–16 again.*

What verse describes an aspect of Christ that you would like to experience more deeply?

Take a few minutes to meditate and pray about the verse. Ask Jesus to reveal himself to you in this way. Journal anything that comes to your heart during your prayer time. Expect that God will continue to reveal this verse to you more fully in the near future as well.

♥ SHARE GOD'S HEART

The context of chapter five in the song gives an interesting perspective for sharing God's heart with those close to us. These verses contain one of the most vivid descriptions of Jesus and his love and devotion to his people in all of Scripture. This exaltation of the Bridegroom occurs in one of the darkest hours for the Shulamite. She had been hurt by her fellow brethren. She felt lost from her Beloved. And yet she took the opportunity to praise him to all who would listen.

- *Next time you find yourself in a situation where you feel like you have been treated unfairly, remember this lesson from the Shulamite in chapter five. Perhaps one of the greatest opportunities for evangelism in your life will occur during a time of persecution. Follow her example and share his goodness and faithfulness with all who will listen.*

Talking It Out

1. What have you learned from the Shulamite's journey in this lesson that is helpful to your own?

2. Have you ever experienced an invitation from the Gethsemane Man to join him in intercession? Share what you were interceding for and what that experience was like.

3. Have you had a spiritual season where you felt lost from your Beloved? Or abused by spiritual leaders? How did you again find the One your soul longs for? What ministered to you in your healing journey?

4. Review the "Ten-fold Description of the Bridegroom" together. Have each person choose one attribute from the list and share how Jesus has revealed himself to them in that way. Then share the attribute that you would most like to experience more of.

5. What have you learned in this lesson about being a healthy spiritual leader? What aspects of Christ's leadership would you like to emulate? What did you learn in this lesson that you would like to bring into your church community?

LESSON 10

Arising like the Dawn

(6:1–10)

The beginning of this lesson is a continuance of the scene from the end of chapter five in the song. The Shulamite experienced a severe trauma in her life through the abuse of spiritual leaders. She felt lost from her beloved and could not find him as she searched through the city. In chapter four she declared that she would go to the mountain of myrrh with him, the mountain of suffering love. In the last chapter, she tasted the spices of this mountain. In a beautiful response, she caught the attention of the brides-to-be when she chose to praise the goodness of her beloved and all the traits that she adored in him.

- *Before beginning the lesson, read Song of Songs 6:1–10 to understand the overall context. What verses or phrases stood out to you? Why?*

Brides-to-be Join the Search

- *Read 6:1.*

    How did the brides-to-be describe the Shulamite, even though she must have been bruised and disheveled?

    What did the brides-to-be long for?

    How did they plan to find the Bridegroom-King?

SHARE GOD'S HEART

The story of the Shulamite teaches us a lesson in the difference between those who lead their flock to the Bridegroom and those who cause harm to her instead. John the Baptist referred to himself as the friend of the Bridegroom. His calling in life was to point others to the coming Messiah.

- *Read John 3:27–36.*

    To whom does the bride belong (v. 29)?

For what does the friend of the Bridegroom listen (v. 29)?

From where does the Bridegroom come and speak (v. 31)?

What words does he speak (v. 34)?

- *Now consider yourself as a friend of the Bridegroom.
  Take note of any names that come to mind as you ponder
  these questions.*

  Who is the Messiah coming for in your life?

  To whom does he want to reveal himself?

  Who will follow you as you seek after Jesus?

How can you be a friend of the Bridegroom in their lives? Ask God to show you specific strategies for sharing his goodness with them.

Found in His Garden

• *Read Song of Songs 6:2–3, including the TPT footnote for verse 2.*

> *How did the Shulamite respond to the question, "Where may we find him?"*

> *Considering the declarations of 5:1, where was "his garden"?*

> *According to 6:2, what was the Bridegroom-King doing in his garden?*

> *How did the Shulamite describe their relationship?*

As the Shulamite answered the question of brides-to-be, she found her Beloved. He was in his garden, and his garden was her heart. This verse marks the beginning of a new reality for the Shulamite, as she would not lose him again. She would always be able to find him in his garden because she was now assured that his garden was within her innermost being.

Glory Within

- *Let's look at a passage of Scripture that describes what it means for Christ to live within us. Read Colossians 1:15–20, including the TPT footnotes.*

  What does Christ reveal to us (v. 15)?

  How does this passage describe the authority of Christ (v. 16)?

  What satisfies God in Christ (v. 19)?

- *Read Colossians 1:21–23, including the TPT footnotes.*

  How was the distance removed between us and Christ so we could dwell in his presence (vv. 21–22)?

  How does the Father see us (vv. 21–22)?

- *Read Colossians 1:26–29, including the TPT footnotes.*

  What is the divine mystery that has been concealed for generations but is now revealed (v. 27)?

  What message did Paul want every believer to understand (v. 28–29)?

- *Read Colossians 2:6–10, including the TPT footnotes.*

  In what should we continue to grow deeper (v. 6)?

Of whom should we beware (v. 8)?

How does verse 9 describe Christ?

Where do we find our completeness (v. 10)?

What overflows within us (v. 10)?

This portion of Scripture shows the completion of God within Christ and the completion of Christ within us. It is truly a profound mystery, one that the Shulamite was grasping in Song of Songs 6:2. She would not lose track of her beloved again. The spiritual reality of life-union had taken hold within her.

A Radiant City

• *Read Song of Songs 6:4, including the TPT footnotes.*

> *To what did the Bridegroom-King compare the Shulamite's beauty?*

According to footnote 'b,' what is this radiant city?

What has the bride done to the heart of the Bridegroom-King?

In his sermon entitled "The Church as She Should Be," Charles Spurgeon wrote the following about this verse:

> Though the words before us are allegorical, and the whole song is crowded with metaphor and parable, yet the teaching is plain enough in this instance; it is evident that the Divine Bridegroom gives his bride a high place in his heart, and to him, whatever she may be to others, she is fair, lovely, comely, beautiful, and in the eyes of his love without a spot. Moreover, even to him there is not only a beauty of a soft and gentle kind in her, but a majesty, a dignity in her holiness, in her earnestness, in her consecration...She is every inch a queen: her aspect in the sight of her beloved is majestic.[50]

THE BACKSTORY

The Bridegroom-King compared the beauty of the Shulamite in 6:4 to two cities: Tirzah and Jerusalem. (The cities are named in the Hebrew text of this verse.)

Tirzah was a Canaanite city in northern Israel that was conquered by Joshua (Joshua 12:24). It was in the land of the tribe of Manasseh. During the time of Solomon, it was considered the most beautiful city in the north. After the death of Solomon, it became the capital of the northern kingdom of Israel under Jeroboam.[51]

There is another interesting Bible story about a woman named Tirzah and her sisters in Numbers 27:1–6. Their father died without an heir, and Moses made a decree for the sisters to receive the full inheritance of the father, even though they were women. This is an interesting story to consider in the context of the Shulamite, who is receiving "equal" standing as well.

Jerusalem became the capital of Israel during the reign of King David (2 Samuel 5:6–10), the father of Solomon. David lived in the "fortress of Zion," which he called the "city of David." Solomon lived and reigned in Jerusalem. The temple he built in that city was filled with the shekinah glory of God (1 Kings 6–8).

Brian and Candice Simmons wrote:

> The beautiful city of Tirzah becomes a symbolic picture of how the last day's bride of Christ will appear to the unbelieving Gentile nations. The bride will be beautiful to unbelievers and seen as the pleasing partner of Jesus Christ…Jerusalem's beauty speaks of the beauty of holiness found in worshiping God…God's very presence dwelt over the Holy of Holies in the temple of Jerusalem. The loyal love of the bride is compared to the holy city of Jerusalem, possessing the glory of God.[52]

A Bride, A City

Both the Old and New Testaments contain passages that compare the people of God to a *city* and specifically a city named Jerusalem. Reading them within the context of Song of Songs 6:4 brings an interesting perspective.

• *Read the following passages and journal what each one reveals about the bride of Christ.*

Psalm 46:4–5

Psalm 48:1–14

Matthew 5:14–16

Hebrews 11:10, 16, and 13:14

Revelation 21:2–3, 9–11, 22–27

Undone with Love

- *Read Song of Songs 6:5, including the TPT footnotes.*

  How did the Bridegroom-King describe the Shulamite's eyes?

  How did the Bridegroom-King describe the effect the bride's glance and love have upon him?

  To what did he compare her devotion?

  According to footnote 'd,' what is the meaning of overcome? *(Refer to the study on 4:3 for the symbolism of Rahab in this verse.)*

  According to footnote 'e' for 6:5, what is the literal Hebrew for "yielded sacrifice"? (Refer to the study on 4:1 for more explanation of this phrase.)

Shining and Unique

• *Read 6:6–9, including the TPT footnotes.*

> *According to the footnote for verse 6, what do the teeth represent?*

> *What did the Shulamite's cheeks reveal to her beloved?*

> *According to the footnote for verse 8, how many could the Bridegroom-King have chosen from?*

> *What six attributes did he use to describe his beloved dove?*

> *How did others celebrate her?*

- *Read Colossians 1:28–29.*

  What did Paul describe as the truth he is passionately laboring to bring to every believer?

  What is the response of your heart when you read this passage?

🔮 EXPERIENCE GOD'S HEART

This section of the song is like reading a love letter from God straight to your heart. Let's not miss the words he is speaking to us because we are studying and analyzing. Take time to reflect and journal your response to each paraphrased expression below. Are you able to receive these words from his heart? Does it feel like too much? Do you feel worthy of his love and praise? Whatever the response of your heart, write it down.

- *When I look at you, I see my dwelling place (Song of Songs 6:4).*

- *You are more pleasing than any pleasure, more delightful than any delight (v. 4).*

- *You ravish my heart (v. 4).*

- *I have no strength to resist you (v. 4).*

- *I adore your passionate eyes (v. 5).*

- *My heart is undone when you turn your gaze upon me (v. 5).*

- *I am overcome and held captive by your love (v. 5).*

- *Your yielded devotion means so much to me (v. 5).*

- *You are taking my truth deeply within you (v. 6).*

- *I love your passion for me (v. 7).*

- *I choose you! You are not second best (v. 8).*

- *You are unique (v. 9).*

- *You are without equal (v. 9).*

- *You are beyond compare (v. 9).*

- *You are perfect (v. 9).*

- *You are my favorite (v. 9).*

- *You are blessed (v. 9).*

Pray to receive his love more fully as you grow and mature in him.

Arising like the Dawn

• *Read verse 10.*

> *As what did the bride arise?*

> *How fair was she?*

> *How brilliant was she?*

> *What was astonishing to behold about her?*

> *What did the banners represent?*

🄷 WORD WEALTH

Let's pause on this verse and consider the tapestry that has been woven thread by thread through the song. The contrast of darkness and light in relation to the bride is a significant theme in the song. Look at the following verses again, considering them as one storyline woven together.

- *In 1:5, she says, "Jerusalem maidens, in this _____ _____..."*

- *In 1:8, he says, "Listen, my _____ one."*

- *In 1:12, "the sweet fragrance of [her] spikenard _____ the _____."*

- *In 1:16, "Our resting place is...like a green forest meadow bathed in _____."*

- *In 2:7, he admonishes the maidens to not disturb her until "she is ready to _____."*

- *In 2:10, his invitation to the bride begins with "_____, my dearest."*

- *In 2:13, he asks, "Can you not discern this _____ _____ of destiny _____ _____ around you?"*

- *In 2:13, he invites her again, "_____, my love, my beautiful companion...now is the time to _____ and come away with me."*

- *In 2:14, he hides her "in the secret stairway of the _____."*

- *In 2:14, he says, "Let me see your _____ face."*

- *In 2:17, what is her excuse to not go with him? "But until the_____ springs to life and the shifting _____ of fear disappear...until the new _____ fully _____..."*

- In 3:1, "_____ after _____" she tosses in bed.
- In 3:2, she says, "So I must _____ in search of him."
- In 3:5, he adjures the maidens again to not disturb her "until she is ready to _____."
- In 3:8, the champions defend the king and fiancée "from every terror of the _____."
- In 4:6, she vows, "Until the _____ disappears and the _____ has fully come, in spite of _____ and fears..."
- In 4:9, "the graces of righteousness [are] _____ upon [her]."
- In 4:13–14, what does spikenard represent? (see the TPT footnote) _____
- In 5:2, he came to her "in the _____ of _____."
- In 5:2, he invites her to "_____, my love...Will you receive me this _____ _____?...I need you this _____ to _____ and come be with me...My flawless one, will you _____?...I have spent myself for you throughout the _____ _____."
- In 5:5, she says, "My spirit _____."
- In 5:6, she says, "I will _____ and search for him."
- In 5:10, "He _____ in dazzling splendor."
- In 6:4, he says, "I see a _____ city."
- In 6:6, he describes, "The _____ of [her] spirit..."
- In 6:10, he says, "Look at you now— _____ as the _____ of the _____, fair as the _____ moon, _____ and _____ as the _____ in all its strength."

- *After considering the "arise" and "shine" language in so many verses throughout the song, how would you describe the triumph of his description of her in 6:10?*

This series of Scripture passages shows the Shulamite's profound journey from darkness to light. The bride was initially held back because of her fear of the dark. In 4:6, she overcame that fear and went to the mountain of suffering love with him. After emerging victorious from her time of testing, she arose like the dawning of a new day. This new day broke forth as she walked into her destiny. She was a radiant city on a hill, whose light was no longer hidden.

◐ DIGGING DEEPER

The language of the bride "arising like the dawn" is not unique to the Song of Songs. A number of other Scripture verses describe the bride of Christ in this context. Let's look at some of them.

Psalm 110:3, "Your people will be your love offerings. In the day of your mighty power you will be exalted, and in the brightness of your holy ones you will shine as an army arising from the womb of the dawn, anointed with the dew of your youth!"

- *How does this verse describe God's people?*

- *How is this similar to the Shulamite climbing the mountain of myrrh?*

- *From where did the army of holy ones arise?*

Isaiah 58:8 and 10 say: "Then my favor will bathe you in sunlight until you are like the dawn bursting through a dark night. And then suddenly your healing will manifest. You will see your righteousness march out before you, and the glory of YAHWEH will protect you from all harm!...and if you offer yourselves in compassion for the hungry and relieve those in misery, then your dawning light will rise in the darkness and your gloom will turn into noonday splendor!"

- *What parallels can you identify between this passage and the Shulamite's journey?*

- *This verse says, "If you offer yourselves in compassion for the hungry." How does this echo within the Shulamite's journey?*

Isaiah 60:1–3 state: "Rise up in splendor and be radiant, for your light has dawned, and Yahweh's glory now streams from you! Look carefully! Darkness blankets the earth, and thick clouds covers the nations, but Yahweh arises upon you and the brightness of his glory appears over you! Nations will be attracted to your radiant light and kings to the sunrise-glory of your new day."

- *What other parallels can you identify between these verses in Isaiah and the Shulamite journey?*

Isaiah 62:1–2 reveals: "For Zion's sake, how can I keep silent? For Jerusalem's sake, how can I remain quiet? I will keep interceding until her righteousness breaks forth like the blazing light of dawn and her salvation like a burning torch! Nations will see your victory-vindication and every king will witness your blinding radiance! You will be called by a brand-new name, given to you from the mouth of Yahweh himself."

- *How does the intercession of Yahweh in this verse compare to the words of the Shepherd-King in the Song of Songs?*

In Ephesians 5:8–9 and 14, the apostle Paul says: "Once your life was full of sin's darkness, but now you have the very light of our Lord shining through you because of your union with him. Your mission is to live as children flooded with his revelation-light! And the supernatural fruits of his light will be seen in you—goodness, righteousness, and truth…'Arise, you sleeper! Rise up from your coffin and the Anointed One will shine his light into you!'"

- *What other parallels do you see between these verses and the Shulamite journey?*

Talking It Out

1. What have you learned from the Shulamite's journey in this lesson that is helpful to your own?

2. Have you tried any of the *Share God's Heart* activities yet with friends or family? If so, describe your experiences with one another. If not, discuss what is holding you back and pray together for encouragement.

3. Sometimes believers can feel a gap between what they read in Scripture and what they experience in their day-to-day life. As you consider the love of Jesus and his pursuit of you, would you say that you experience that in your life? If so, what does his love look like and feel like in your life? If not, why do you think his love for you still feels distant?

4. What inspires you about the destiny of the bride of Christ to arise like the dawn as a blessing to the nations? How would you like to see that light break forth in yourself or your church community?

LESSON 11

The Harvest

(6:11–7:13)

At this point in the Shulamite story, our bride had risen in her glory. As Watchman Nee wrote in his commentary, "Her shadows have fled away; there is no further barrier between her and the Lord. She enters into a life without barrier. Although it is not yet high noon, it is nevertheless morning. Her future is as bright as the morning light, and her hope is as promising as the morning."[53]

The time of trial and testing had ended for the Shulamite. She will spend the balance of the book pursuing her life destiny with her king.

- *Before beginning the lesson, read Song of Songs 6:11– 7:13 to understand the overall context. What verses or phrases struck you? Why?*

Budding Vines

• *Read 6:11.*

    Where did the Shulamite go at the beginning of the verse?

    What do you think the "orchards of the king" and the "budding vines" represent?

    What was the bride looking for in the orchards?

    What was she looking for in the vines?

    The Hebrew text says she had gone to the "nut orchard" and the "vineyards in the valley" to see whether the "pomegranates were in bloom." She had gone to the local church to see if the fruit of the Bridegroom's love was blooming in their midst. Could she find the new blossoms of love breaking forth in the bride of Christ?

His Royal Chariot

• *Read verse 12, including the footnote.*

What transported the Shulamite?

Where did her desire bring her?

Where were they sitting together, and where did they go?

What does the footnote say about this verse?

 WORD WEALTH

As we discovered in the TPT footnote, this is considered the most difficult verse of the Song of Songs to translate. The literal Hebrew is translated "the chariot of Ammi-nadib." Some commentaries believe Ammi-nadib was the name of one of Solomon's chariot drivers. *The JPS Bible Commentary* says, "this chariot belongs to a 'nobleman of the people'…[or] Construed figuratively, it tells us that this chariot is elegant—finely tooled and appointed (like the palanquin of Solomon, 3:10)."[54]

This verse describes the lovers being carried up together into a heavenly realm. Elijah was carried up into a heavenly realm in a fiery chariot (2 Kings 2:11). He declared, "My father, my father! The chariots of Israel and its horsemen!" (v. 12 ESV).[55]

Dance with Angels

• *Read Song of Songs 6:13, including the footnote.*

What did the brides-to-be ask of the Shulamite?

How did she respond?

How did the Bridegroom-King describe the Shulamite's dance?

Sandaled Feet

The next chapter in the song celebrates the victorious bride walking into the fullness of her calling and gifts. Most of chapter seven is a declaration by the Bridegroom-King of all the growth he observed in the life of the Shulamite Bride. In chapter four he described her from head to toe. In chapter seven he describes her from toe to head.

• *Read 7:1.*

> *Where was the Shulamite bride located at the beginning of this verse?*

> *How did he describe her feet?*

> *What was the good news her feet were bringing?*

> *How did he describe her status in his kingdom?*

> *How did he describe her walk?*

> *In the last line of the verse, how did he describe her?*

- *Read Ephesians 2:10, including the TPT footnotes.*

  How does this verse compare to Song of Songs 7:1?

  How long has our destiny of good works been planned?

Womb of Wheat

- *Read Song of Songs 7:2–3.*

  What was flowing from the innermost being of the Shulamite?

  What was growing in her womb?

  How did the Bridegroom say she would nurture their sons and daughters?

The John 7:38 reality had taken hold in her life. Her innermost being flowed with the power of the Holy Spirit. Her sandaled feet of good news were creating a new generation of sons and daughters in the kingdom. She partnered with the Bridegroom-King to grow his family.

• *Read John 1:12–13, including the TPT footnotes.*

   How are new children brought into the family of God?

   Into what realm are they born?

 # SHARE GOD'S HEART

As the bride of Christ, we are integral to the family of God growing. The sandaled feet of the bride deliver the message of God's love to the world.

• *Have you considered yourself equipped with the good news of the gospel of the kingdom? Or has that always felt to you like a job for missionaries or evangelists?*

- *Ask the Holy Spirit to show you one person in your life who is ready to receive the message of God's love for the world (John 3:16–17). Ideally, this should be an unbeliever.*

- *Take action to share your heart with them. If they show interest in learning more about God, invite them to study the Bible together or attend a church service.*

Light on a Hill

- *Read Song of Songs 7:4, including the TPT footnote.*

  How did the Bridegroom describe the Shulamite's life now?

How does this verse compare to Matthew 5:14–16?

How did he describe her eyes?

According to the footnote, what does "the pools of Heshbon" mean?

What was the value of the Shulamite's discernment?

Crowned with Love

• *Read Song of Songs 7:5.*

What expression of love crowned the Shulamite?

How did the Bridegroom-King describe her thoughts?

What impact did her beauty have upon him?

🚦 THE EXTRA MILE

In their commentary, Brian and Candice Simmons categorize ten attributes of the risen bride from Song of Songs 7:1–5. They introduce this section by writing, "These ten prophecies will be fulfilled in the church before Jesus returns. They are descriptions of virtues and strengths that He will supernaturally deposit within her. Essentially, what follows is a practical definition of godliness and virtue that will arise like a shining light within the church."[56] The ten attributes are:

1. Her good-news shoes (7:1)

2. Her graceful walk (v. 1)

3. Her inward life (vv. 2–3)

4. Giving birth to a harvest (vv. 2–3)

5. Her power to nurture others (vv. 2–3)

6. Her determination (v. 4)

7. Her clear revelation (v. 4)

8. Her spiritual discernment (v. 4)

9. Her pure thoughts (v. 5)

10. Her dedication to Jesus (v. 5)

For a deeper study of this portion of Scripture, read pages 198–206 in *The Sacred Journey*.

Vineyard of Love

• *Read Song of Songs 7:6–7.*

> *How did the Bridegroom describe the Shulamite's beauty?*

> *Of all her delights, what was the greatest to the Bridegroom?*

> *How did the Shulamite now stand?*

> *What did she share with her Beloved?*

The bride and Bridegroom were now sharing an abundant vineyard of love. In these final chapters of the song, we see the fruit of life-union coming forth in her life.

• *Read John 15:5–8.*

> *How did the Shulamite's life reveal this passage in action?*

What is the fruit of a vineyard of love, living in life-union with the Bridegroom?

• *Read Song of Songs 7:8–9.*

What did the Bridegroom-King decree?

What did he intend to possess?

What would he drink?

How did he describe his bride's kisses of love?

What did her kisses awaken?

Song of Songs 7:8 includes a phrase in Hebrew that is literally translated, "Your breath like a fragrance of apples."[57] The Shulamite started eating the apples in 2:3 when she came to rest under the shade of his grace. She continued to eat of his promises in 2:5. Now her breath smells like apples because of this lifestyle of living within his grace and promises. The words from her mouth reflect this reality.

🔶 EXPERIENCE GOD'S HEART

Missionary Hudson Taylor wrote the following about Song of Songs 7:6–9 in his commentary:

> How wondrous the grace that has made the bride of Christ to be all this to her Beloved! Upright as the palm, victorious, and evermore fruitful as she grows heavenward; gentle and tender as the Vine, self-forgetful and self-sacrificing, not merely bearing fruit in spite of adversity, but bearing her richest fruits through it;—feasting on her Beloved, as she rests beneath His shade, and thereby partaking of His fragrance;— what has grace not done for her! And what must be her joy in finding, ever more fully, the satisfaction of the glorious Bridegroom in the lowly wild flower He has made His bride, and beautified with His own graces and virtues![58]

Let's pause and consider what the fruit of Jesus, the True Vine, has produced in us, the branches.

- *How is the victory of heaven evident within your story?*

- *What fruit has God brought forth through adversity in your life?*

- *How would you describe God's grace at work in your life?*

- *Pray for an increased ability to receive the joy and satisfaction of the Bridegroom. Ask him to reveal to your heart how he sees you and his love for you. Journal anything the Holy Spirit reveals to you during this prayer time.*

Come Away with Me

• *Read 7:10–12, including the TPT footnotes.*

What was the Shulamite assured of now?

According to the footnote for verse 10, what does the word yadiyad *mean?*

Where were all the Bridegroom's desires fulfilled?

Who made the invitation to "Come away" in verse 11?

How was this different from previous invitations to "Come away" mentioned in 2:10 and 2:13?

Where did the Shulamite bride invite her lover to go with her?

What did she say they would show the people they find in these places?

In 7:12, she also invited him to arise and go where with her?

According to footnote 'b' for 7:12, what do the vineyards represent?

What were the lovers looking to see in the vineyards?

What did they expect to discover there?

What did the Shulamite promise to display in the vineyards?

According to footnote 'c' for verse 12, what do pomegranates represent?

In this section of Scripture, the Shulamite invited the Bridegroom-King to come away with her. This shows the progression in the relationship of her becoming his true partner. Here he followed the desire of her heart to share their love with the faraway places as well as the church.

• *Read John 15:14–17, including the TPT footnotes.*

How did the Shulamite's journey reveal this passage in action?

What was Jesus' parting command in this passage?

- *Read Matthew 28:16–20 and Acts 1:4–8.*

   How did Jesus commission his disciples in their final time together?

   What is the role of the Holy Spirit in going to the remotest places to share the good news?

 DIGGING DEEPER

One of the greatest examples of taking Christ to the faraway fields is found in the life of Hudson Taylor. Hudson Taylor was born in Barnsley, England, in 1832 to a Yorkshire Methodist family. Several generations of his family before him were ministers for God. Before Hudson was born, his parents consecrated his life to God as a missionary, praying that he would someday bring the gospel to China. They did not tell him of this prayer until after he returned from his first trip to China.[59]

At the age of fifteen, Hudson received Christ into his heart, and shortly after that, he had a spiritual encounter with God in which he devoted his life to the work of Jesus. In his autobiography, he wrote: "The presence of God became unutterably real and blessed; and though but a child under sixteen, I remember stretching myself on the ground, and lying there silent before Him with unspeakable awe and unspeakable joy. For what service I was accepted I knew not; but a deep consciousness that I was no longer my own took possession of me, which has never since been effaced."[60]

By the age of twenty-one, Taylor left on his first missionary journey to mainland China. During his lifetime, he made ten ocean crossings from England to China, spending between four to five years on the water alone. When he arrived in China, he became acutely aware of the importance of speaking the language and immersing himself in the culture. He chose a radically different approach than other missionaries of his time. He resided in unsecured neighborhoods with locals and integrated into the culture. He adopted Chinese dress, shaved his head, and grew a pigtail in the traditional local fashion.[61]

Hudson Taylor is widely considered one of the most significant missionaries in Christian history, and he is credited with opening China to the gospel. He founded China Inland Mission. By the time of his death in 1905, over twenty-five thousand locals had converted to Christianity. They had 825 missionaries operating in eighteen provinces. The organization, OMF International, is still operating today from Singapore.[62]

Hudson Taylor lived a life of dependence upon God to supply his every need. This lifestyle began even as a teenager. He followed the model of the apostles in Acts, being sent forth with nothing and relying upon God to provide. He also cherished his union with Christ. His life's work was fueled by his abiding in union with Christ.

He wrote his own commentary on the Song of Songs, entitled *Union and Communion*. In an explanation of 8:3, he wrote, "I would give Thee my best, and yet would myself seek all my rest and satisfaction in Thee...There is nothing sweeter to the Bridegroom or to the bride than this hallowed and unhindered communion."[63] His commentary is a short but profound work that every serious student of the Song of Songs should explore.[64]

Storehouse of Love

- *Read Song of Songs 7:13.*

    What fruit was in bloom?

    What did the fruit send forth?

    What did the bride and Bridegroom find at their doors?

    Who had stored them there?

    What term of endearment does the Shulamite use for the Bridegroom-King at the end of this verse?

This is another full-circle passage in the song. The Shulamite was revived as she sat and ate the apples under his shady tree in 2:3. Now the apples of their love were in bloom for the nations to eat. The fragrance was sent out upon the wind. The spring that came forth in her life starting in chapter two was now going forth to all who were enticed by the fragrance of love in the air.

The world is hungry to know a God who loves them. The abundance of the Shulamite's life will bring the nations to him as his inheritance.

Talking It Out

1. What have you learned from the Shulamite's journey in this lesson that is helpful to your own?

2. What is an area of promise or inheritance in your spiritual walk with God? What would make the angel camps dance in celebration over your life if you started to walk toward it?

3. Do you feel equipped to share the gospel with unbelievers? If the answer is no, what would make you feel more comfortable? If the answer is yes, could you equip other sisters and brothers in Christ to share the good news more frequently?

4. Tell about a time of adversity in your life that produced beautiful fruit in the kingdom. How did God or other believers minister to you during that time? How did you grow in your life-union with God during that experience?

5. If you could invite Jesus to either a faraway place or a local group of believers to bring the message of love, what would you choose? Have you ever been on a short-term or long-term mission journey? Share your experiences with one another.

LESSON 12

The Fiery Seal of Eternal Love

(8:1–14)

The final chapter of the Song of Songs is an expression of eternal love. The Shulamite healed and grew throughout her journey with her Bridegroom. Everything she cried out for in chapter one occurred. She found the secret garden within where she would never lose her Beloved again. Her garden was thriving and became a table for the nations. The bride and Bridegroom went to faraway places together as well as to the local church. In this final lesson, let's enjoy the overflowing abundance of their love.

- *Before beginning the lesson, read 8:1–14 to understand the overall context. What verses or phrases stood out to you? Why?*

The Holy Sanctuary

• *Read verses 1–2.*

   What was the Shulamite bride's desire (v. 1)?

   Where did she long to bring the Bridegroom-King (v. 2)?

   What did she want to serve him?

   How long did the Shulamite want to drink from the cup of bliss?

Verse 1 expresses the bride's desire to share their love publicly. The original Hebrew says that she wished he were her brother so she could kiss him in public. In the cultural context when the song was written, it would have been scandalizing to kiss a beloved in public but socially acceptable to kiss her brother.[65]

The Shulamite transformed from an inner vineyard that was in disarray and unproductive to one that was producing spiced wine. This was the costliest of wines. In the case of the Shulamite, what was the cost of attaining the spiced wine? She had to go with him to the mountain of myrrh and the hill of incense. Her garden became fragrant with all the choice spices after she said yes to him in 4:6. Now that her garden was fragrant with spices, she had spiced wine from her vineyard to share with him. This was her "cup of bliss."

🔡 WORD WEALTH

These first few verses in chapter eight include a play on words that harkens back to the very beginning of the song. She said she longs to kiss him in the open where all can see and then drink their fill of wine together from the cup of bliss. In 1:2, the journey began with her calling out for a kiss: "Let him smother me with kisses...I drink them in like the sweetest wine!" (Refer to the TPT footnote in 1:2 for the explanation of the wordplay between *to kiss* and *take a drink of wine*.)

These verses in 8:1–2 include the same play on words in the Hebrew, just as we saw in the first chapter. *The JPS Bible Commentary* says, "This sequence of verbs stresses her desire to bring the beloved home to the elixir of love. These actions are correlated by a pun. The list begins with *'eshaqekha* ('I would kiss you,' v. 1) and ends with *'ashqekha* ('I would let your drink'; literally, 'I would slake you'...)."[66]

Resting in Love

• *Read 8:3–4.*

How was the Bridegroom-King holding his bride?

Where were they resting?

Compare 8:3–4 to 2:6–7 and identify the differences.

Out of Her Desert

• *Read 8:5.*

From where was the Shulamite arising?

To whom was she clinging?

How does this verse compare to 3:6? What progression does it show?

From where did the Bridegroom-King awaken her? What verse was he recalling in this statement (hint: go to chapter two)?

What did resting under the apple tree and eating his apples represent in chapter two?

How did he awaken her innermost being?

What did she birth?

Brian and Candice Simmons wrote of this verse:

> The day will come when all that is within you will be lost in Him forever. Song of Songs 8:5 is your destiny. The Lord's strategy throughout your life has been to produce in you an attitude of total dependency on Him (Jer. 9:23). Loving hearts will find no confidence in self but will discover an endless source of life in Him (2 Cor. 3:5–6). As we mesh our hearts with His, we absorb His life. It bleeds through...We must keep leaning harder and harder into Him until it is asked with amazement, "Who is this, clinging to his or her Lover?"[67]

 EXPERIENCE GOD'S HEART

In their commentary, Brian and Candice Simmons also share five ways that we can lean upon our Beloved Jesus:[68]

1. To be saved from sin

2. To live above the power of sin

3. To walk in emotional wholeness

4. To receive guidance and direction for our lives

5. To be provided for and loved

• *Lean into your beloved Bridegroom as you consider the following:*

> *In which of the five areas listed above would you like to be more dependent upon God?*

> *Pause and spend time in meditative prayer. Share your heart with your Beloved for more intimacy with him on this issue and listen for the sharing of his heart in return. Journal what you experienced.*

Sealed with Love

• *Read Song of Songs 8:6, including the TPT footnotes.*

> *How did the Bridegroom fasten his beloved to his heart?*

> *To what did she become a prisoner?*

> *According to footnote 'a,' what is an alternate meaning of the Hebrew word for "seal"?*

> *What did the Bridegroom-King say was stronger than the chains of death?*

> *According to footnote 'b,' what is an alternate translation of "passion"?*

> *From where did the all-consuming fire come?*

According to footnote 'c,' what is the full meaning of "a most vehement flame"?

According to footnote 'c,' who is "Yah"?

According to the same footnote, what is another translation of the last phrase of this verse?

This is one of the most quoted verses from the Song of Songs. This verse is packed with meaning, and the study of it could become an entire book on its own. Let's spend some time examining what this verse expresses from the heart of God.

ⓝ WORD WEALTH

In the TPT footnote for Song of Songs 8:6, we find that the Hebrew word for "seal" can also be translated as "prison cell." The Shulamite became a prisoner of the Bridegroom's love. She was sealed within his love forevermore.

The apostle Paul used similar wording in some of his writings. In Ephesians 4:1 and Romans 1:1, he described himself as a prisoner of the Lord. The TPT footnote for Romans 1:1 says, "The Greek word *doulos* signifies more than a servant; it is one who has chosen to serve a master out of love, bound with cords so strong that it could only be severed by death."[69]

This concept of a servant who chooses to forever serve a master out of love comes from an ancient Hebrew custom. Read Exodus 21:5–6 and Deuteronomy 15:16–17. Both passages describe an opportunity for a slave to be set free, but they choose instead to stay and serve in their master's house for the rest of their lives. The sign of this service was a pierced ear.

DIGGING DEEPER

Some translations describe the love of the Bridegroom-King for his Shulamite bride in Song of Songs 8:6 with the words "as strong as death" and "as jealous as the grave."

- *Read the following verses and note what each reveals about the finality of the grave and the hope we have in Jesus.*

  Job 7:9; 14:12

  Psalm 89:48

  Isaiah 26:14

  Ecclesiastes 7:1

Romans 5:12–17

1 Corinthians 15:20–22

Hebrews 9:27–28

What could be more final in life than death? How jealous is the grave for every life that walks on earth? God compares his love to the most final, complete, and persistent experiences for every human on earth (perhaps with the exceptions of Enoch and Elijah). You have as much chance of escaping the pursuit of God's love as you do the grave. His love will chase you through Sheol and raise you up to be seated next to him. His love will hold you for all eternity. This is the love the Bridegroom described to the Shulamite, his beloved bride.

Rivers and Floods

• *Read Song of Songs 8:7.*

> *What cannot extinguish this flame of Yah?*

> *What extreme event would not quench the burning fire within the Shulamite?*

What would this fire consume?

What could stop it?

What would happen as she yielded to it?

• *In the Old Testament, there is a story of a fire that eats up the water in its path. Read 1 Kings 18:20–40.*

   What does verse 24 say about God's answer to the call of Elijah?

   How does verse 35 describe the amount of water on the altar?

   In verse 38, what did the fire consume?

In verse 39, what did the people declare in response?

- *A few other verses in the Bible describe God as an unrelenting fire. Read each one and journal what they reveal.*

    Deuteronomy 4:24

    Deuteronomy 9:3

    Hebrews 12:29

Enclosed in Cedar

- *Read Song of Songs 8:8–10.*

    Why did the Shulamite's brothers guard her?

Until when did they guard her?

How did the Bridegroom-King say he would protect her?

How is the "wall of cedar boards" an echo of 1:17?

Now that she was mature, did she still need their protection?

Where did her protection come from now?

How did she become a protection for others who are still immature?

How did her beloved see her?

What did she bring him?

Where did she find favor?

Vineyard of Love

• *Read verses 11–13, including the TPT footnotes.*

Of what was the vineyard of love composed?

According to the footnote for verse 11, what does the king's vineyard represent?

According to the same footnote, what does Baal-hamon *mean? (Baal-hamon is the location of the vineyard in the original Hebrew.)*

What did the caretakers of the vineyard give the king?

From her own vineyard, what did the Shulamite bride give the king?

According to footnote 'a' for verse 12, what is another way "all the glory" can be translated?

According to the same footnote, what is the significance of the number one thousand?

In the last half of verse 12, what did the Shulamite give those who serve the king?

What did they watch over?

This parable at the end of the song portrays the accountability of God's people. They were entrusted with the stewardship of a vineyard that was meant to produce a harvest for the King of kings.

• *Read Matthew 25:14–30, including the TPT footnotes.*

What does this parable teach about stewardship for God?

According to the footnote for verse 15, what was a yearly tribute to King Solomon?

♥ SHARE GOD'S HEART

The parable of the vineyard of love describes a two-fold vineyard. First it describes the vineyard of the church, the body of Christ. The caretakers or the spiritual leaders oversaw this. The second description of the vineyard within this passage is the personal vineyard of the Shulamite. From her personal vineyard, she gave all the glory (or one thousand shekels). She then gave double honor (or two hundred shekels) from her vineyard to the caretakers of the body of Christ. She was tithing a double portion of her abundance or glory to the church (see Numbers 18:21, 24).

As you mature in your walk of faith, consider the following:

• *How do you share your abundance or glory with the King? (Don't be limited by financial resources when considering this question.)*

• *How do you share your abundance or glory with his church? (Again, don't be limited to financial resources when considering this question.)*

- *Ask the Holy Spirit to reveal the "talents" he has given you that you can use for his glory.*

- *Ask the Holy Spirit to reveal where you should share your talents or resources in the body of Christ.*

 THE EXTRA MILE

Just as the Song of Songs describes the victorious bride of Christ, so does Proverbs 31:10–31, which depicts "The Radiant Bride." The TPT footnote for 31:10 says:

> Starting with verse 10 through the end of the book, we have a Hebrew acrostic poem. It is alphabetical in structure, with each of the twenty-two verses beginning with a consecutive Hebrew letter of the alphabet. The implication is that the perfections of this woman would exhaust the entire language. The subject is the perfect bride, the virtuous woman. This woman is both a picture of a virtuous wife and an incredible

allegory of the end-time victorious bride of
Jesus Christ, full of virtue and grace.[70]

- Read Proverbs 31:10–31, including the TPT footnotes.

    What similarities do you see between the hoped-for
    wife of Proverbs 31 and the Shulamite bride of the
    Song of Songs?

    What differences do you see between the two?

The Divine Duet

- Read Song of Songs 8:13–14.

    How did the Shulamite bride describe their life union (v. 13)?

    Who was listening for the voice of the Bridegroom-King?

In the divine duet, what did they encourage each other toward?

Where did they want to dance?

What would be their forever reality?

How was her prayer of 1:2 answered?

How was her prayer of 1:4 answered?

What happened to the mountains of separation between them?

How did she answer the call to "arise" and "come away" with him?

In the words of Brian and Candice Simmons:

> She has said "I do" to the King. What divine
> partners they make. Wooed and pursued.
> Spinning, twirling, skipping together. It
> is a marriage made in heaven. They are
> bride and Bridegroom forever, like gazelles
> leaping in resurrection power. Their love
> is as innocent as a spring morning, pure
> as a mountain spring. What joy they find
> together on the mountains of fragrant
> spice. Arm in arm they join together in the
> ancient dance before the Ancient of Days.[71]

The victorious bride of Christ will herald his return to the earth. In the words of Revelation 22:17, "'Come,' says the Holy Spirit and the Bride in divine duet. Let everyone who hears this duet join them in saying, 'Come.' Let everyone gripped with spiritual thirst say, 'Come.' And let everyone who craves the gift of living water come and drink it freely. 'Come.'"

Let's join this divine duet!

Talking It Out

1. What have you learned from the Shulamite's journey in this lesson that is helpful to your own?

2. Are you in a wilderness or valley where you must lean on the Beloved to come up and out? What does resting in him look like for you in this season? How do you want to lean more upon the Bridegroom Jesus?

3. Have you ever had an experience with the fire of God's love? An experience where you felt sealed with love? Share your stories with one another. What did God accomplish in you during that time? Pray for one another to have a greater encounter with the passionate fire of Yah.

4. What have you learned about the love of God, specifically for his church and for yourself, through the study of the Song of Songs? In what ways would you like to experience more of God's love? Pray together for the abundant fruit of the study of the Song of Songs to take root in your heart.

Endnotes

1.   Brian Simmons et al., "A Note to Readers," *The Passion Translation: The New Testament with Psalms, Proverbs, and Song of Songs* (Savage, MN: BroadStreet Publishing Group, 2020), ix.

2   Michael Fishbane, *The JPS Bible Commentary: Song of Songs* (Philadelphia, PA: The Jewish Publication Society, 2015), xx-xxi.

3   For a defense of the traditional view of the song's authorship, see Gleason L. Archer, *A Survey of Old Testament Introduction*, revised ed. (Chicago, IL: Moody Press, 2007), chap. 35.

4   Fr. Juan Gonzalez Arintero, *The Song of Songs* (Rockford, IL: Tan Books and Publishers, 1992), 14.

5   Brian and Candice Simmons, *The Sacred Journey* (Racine, WI: Broadstreet Publishing, 2015), 7.

6   Fishbane, *The JPS Bible Commentary: Song of Songs*, xxii.

7   Fishbane, *The JPS Bible Commentary: Song of Songs*, xlvii, l.

8   Mark DelCogliano, *Gregory the Great on The Song of Songs* (Collegeville, MN: Liturgical Press, 2012), 35, 71–72.

9   DelCogliano, *Gregory the Great on The Song of Songs*, 54–55.

10   *The Geneva Bible 1560 Edition* (Peabody, MA: Hendrickson, 2007), 280.

11   C. H. Spurgeon, *The Most Holy Place* (Ross-shire, Great Britain: Christian Focus, 1996), 294–95.

12   J. Hudson Taylor, *Union and Communion: Thoughts on the Song of Solomon* (London, England: The China Inland Mission, 1914).

13   Richard Wurmbrand, *The Sweetest Song* (Basingstoke, Hant, UK: Marshall Pickering, 1988).

14   Fishbane, *The JPS Bible Commentary: Song of Songs*, l.

15   Jeanne Guyon, *Song of Songs* (Jacksonville, FL: SeedSowers, 2017), 1.

16   James Strong, *The Exhaustive Concordance of the Bible* (New York: Abingdon Press, 1890), h5401.

17   Strong, *The Exhaustive Concordance of the Bible, g*5548.

18   Fishbane, *The JPS Bible Commentary: Song of Songs*, 34.

19   Fishbane, *The JPS Bible Commentary: Song of Songs*, xxxiv–xlvii.

20   Taylor, *Union and Communion*, 17.

21   Ralph Gower, *The New Manners and Customs of Bible Times* (Oxford, England: Moody, 2004), 53.

22   Gower, *The New Manners and Customs of Bible Times*, 218.

23   Strong, *The Exhaustive Concordance of the Bible*, h3722.

24   Watchman Nee, *The Song of Songs* (Anaheim, CA: Living Stream Ministry, 1993), 23.

25   Fishbane, *The JPS Bible Commentary: Song of Songs*, 51.

26   Arintero, *The Song of Songs*, 199.

27   Simmons, *The Sacred Journey*, 67.

28   Simmons, *The Sacred Journey*, 78.

29   John 19:30, note 'c,' TPT.

30   Strong, *The Exhaustive Concordance of the Bible*, h7759 and h7999.

31   Simmons, *The Sacred Journey*, 83.

32   Strong, *The Exhaustive Concordance of the Bible*, h4296.

33   Simmons, *The Sacred Journey*, 112–13.

34   Spurgeon, *The Most Holy Place*, 280–81. This short excerpt from his sermon was preached at the Metropolitan Tabernacle in Newington, England, on January 23, 1859. For a deeper study, download the whole sermon and read his perspective on what this verse from the Song of Songs means for a believer in Christ.

35 Simmons, *The Sacred Journey,* 121.
36 Thomas C. Upham, *Life and Religious Opinions and Experience of Madame De La Mothe Guyon* (New York: Harper & Brothers, 1860), 52–53.
37 Guyon, *Song of Songs,* publisher's preface.
38 Wikipedia, s.v. "Jeanne Guyon," last modified on March 5, 2024, https://en.wikipedia.org.
39 Strong, *The Exhaustive Concordance of the Bible,* h0269.
40 Simmons, *The Sacred Journey,* 142.
41 Wurmbrand, *The Sweetest Song,* 164.
42 Wikipedia, s.v. "Richard Wurmbrand," last modified on March 4, 2024, https://en.wikipedia.org.
43 Strong, *The Exhaustive Concordance of the Bible,* h6703, h0122, h0119.
44 Genesis 1:26, note 'c,' TPT.
45 Simmons, *The Sacred Journey,* 168.
46 Simmons, *The Sacred Journey,* 168–74.
47 Simmons, *The Sacred Journey,* 168–74.
48 Simmons, *The Sacred Journey,* 172.
49 Jeremiah 31:20, note 'e,' TPT.
50 Spurgeon, *The Most Holy Place,* 464.
51 Simmons, *The Sacred Journey,* 183.
52 Simmons, *The Sacred Journey,* 183.
53 Nee, *The Song of Songs,* 101.
54 Fishbane, *The JPS Bible Commentary: Song of Songs,* 173.
55 Charles Spurgeon devoted an entire sermon to this verse. It is entitled "The Chariots of Ammi-Nadib." He preached this sermon at the Metropolitan Tabernacle in London, England, on January 1, 1874. You can access the sermon here: https://www.spurgeon.org/resource-library/sermons/the-chariots-of-ammi-nadie/#flipbook.
56 Simmons, *The Sacred Journey,* 199.
57 Fishbane, *The JPS Bible Commentary: Song of Songs,* 190.
58 Taylor, *Union and Communion,* 66.
59 Vance Christie, *Hudson Taylor: Gospel Pioneer to China* (Phillipsburg, NJ: P&R Publishing, 2011), 17–19.
60 J. Hudson Taylor, *Hudson Taylor: The Autobiography of a Man Who Brought the Gospel to China* (Bloomington, MN: Bethany House, 1987), 14–15.
61 Ralph R. Covell and G. Wright Doyle, "J. Hudson Taylor," *Biographical Dictionary of Chinese Christianity,* Global China Center, accessed October 10, 2024, https://bdcconline.net.
62 John Piper, "This Day in History: The Death of Hudson Taylor," Crossway, June 3, 2018, https://www.crossway.org.
63 Taylor, *Union and Communion,* 69.
64 Taylor's *Union and Communion* is part of the public domain and can be easily accessed here: https://ccel.org/ccel/taylor_jh/union/union.i.html.
65 Fishbane, *The JPS Bible Commentary: Song of Songs,* 199.
66 Fishbane, *The JPS Bible Commentary: Song of Songs,* 201.
67 Simmons, *The Sacred Journey,* 226.
68 Simmons, *The Sacred Journey,* 226–27.
69 Romans 1:1, note 'a,' TPT.
70 Proverbs 31:10, note 'a,' TPT.
71 Simmons, *The Sacred Journey,* 248.